P9-CED-688

LADY GI

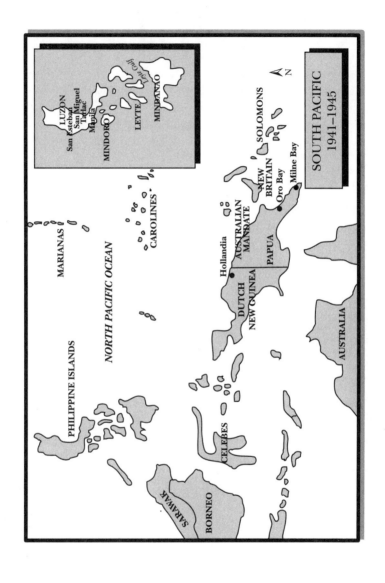

A Woman's War in the South Pacific

LADY GI

Irene J. Brion

✠ The Memoir of Irene Brion ✠

Irene Brion

★
PRESIDIO

To Mom

Copyright © 1997 by Irene J. Brion

Published by Presidio Press
505 B San Marin Drive, Suite 300
Novato, CA 94945-1340

All rights reserved. No part of this book may be reproduced or utilized in any form or by any means, electronic or mechanical, including photocopying, recording, or by any information storage and retrieval systems, without permission in writing from the publisher. Inquiries should be addressed to Presidio Press, 505 B San Marin Drive, Suite 300, Novato, CA 94945-1340.

Library of Congress Cataloging-in-Publication Data

Brion, Irene.
    Lady GI : a woman's war in the South Pacific / Irene Brion.
        p.   cm.
  ISBN: 0-89141-633-1 (hardcover)
  1. Brion, Irene. 2. World War, 1939–1945—Campaigns—Pacific Area. 3. World War, 1939–1945—Personal narratives, American. 4. United States. Army. Women's Army Corps—Biography. 5. Women soldiers—United States—Biography. I. Title.
D767.9.B75   1997
940.54'26—dc21   97-25409
                               CIP

All photos from the Author's collection
Printed in the United States of America

Introduction

In the following account of my experiences in the Women's Army Corps (and its predecessor, the Women's Army Auxiliary Corps) during World War II, I have relied largely upon my memory, assisted by a brief outline of events that I jotted down the first year after the war, letters preserved by Margery Cady and Sue Cross Santa Maria and kindly lent to me, scrapbook items, and photos and shared experiences remembered by several of my fellow Wacs. To avoid the pitfalls inherent in such an approach—memory can be capricious, especially when recalling events that occurred so long ago— I have taken special care to include mainly those incidents that can be verified by the sources mentioned. Dates of letters and information from scrapbook items were particularly useful in placing myriad memories in the best possible chronological order. Photos, many of which I inspected minutely, were valuable in reconstructing details of landscapes and buildings, although I have always found that sensory recollections come easily. The same is true for recalling personal feelings.

Prologue

It was 1943 and my country was fighting for its life in the world's greatest war. I was twenty-three. I'd been following developments with avid interest from the start—especially Dunkirk, the bombing of London, the invasion of Russia, and the bombing of Pearl Harbor. History was happening all around me.

I was vicariously taking part in it, but it never occurred to me that I could participate directly—until one day when I went shopping in Rochester with Mom and my sister Elsie. Women's Army Auxillary Corps (WAAC) recruiters were in the street. At that moment it occurred to Mom, who was patriotic and had no sons to offer to the cause, that she did have an eligible daughter. (Elsie wouldn't have passed the physical—she had phlebitis.) Mom paused and looked at me. Suddenly the idea seemed appealing. I took some of their brochures. Women Accepted for Volunteer Emergency Service (WAVES) was recruiting farther down the street, so I picked up some of their materials too.

By the time I mulled things over, I had come up with four good reasons that clinched my decision to enlist. Foremost were the educational opportunities. The navy was sending people to Smith College and graduating them as officers.

Here was a chance to attend a prestigious school and perhaps take advantage of educational rights for veterans. Second, I wanted desperately to be where the action was. Then there were the limitless opportunities that military life offered—dates and contacts with people from all over the country and from all walks of life. The draft and gas rationing had curtailed the already limited social life of Friendship, the remote village in upstate New York where I was teaching.

Finally, patriotism was in the air, and no one caught a more romanticized case of it than I did. I visualized myself in a uniform, marching amid waving flags into vaguely defined dangers, much like the heroines I'd been reading about since Abraham and George looked down at me from the walls of our one-room district school, challenging me to do or die for my country.

I wanted my family, and especially my mother, to be proud of me. She wouldn't have to be silent when her friends talked about their sons and relatives in the service, and she could hang one of those little banners with a blue star on it in her window. (The banners had a red border on a white background and a blue star for each family member serving in the armed forces.)

In March 1943 I applied to the navy and three weeks later received papers for a physical. These I took to the local doctor, had the physical, and returned the forms. Shortly afterward the navy wrote back saying that I didn't qualify for an officer's commission because I didn't have 20/20 vision. Meanwhile, rumors had gotten around town that I was going into military service. I fell back on the WAAC. Besides, I had heard that the navy was restricted mainly to stateside duty, in such places as Washington, D.C., Chicago, and San Diego, whereas WAACs were sent to all sorts of places, both in the states and overseas. That sounded much more appealing to me. I mailed my application forms to the WAAC recruiting office in Buffalo; they called me in for a physical and soon I found myself raising my right hand. The deed was done.

The day after my return to Friendship, a letter arrived from the navy saying that it had lowered its requirements and I now qualified for a commission. I declined. By that time I was really excited about the WAAC. Because I was teaching, I was permitted to finish the school year and would report on or about July 1.

Official announcement of my acceptance in the WAAC, dated April 22, 1943, informed me of my rank and serial number—Auxiliary Basic A-217606—and directed me and seven others "to proceed to our respective homes and await further orders pertinent to being called to active duty"—by order of Major Morrow and signed by recruiting officer Jeanne P. Gapp. Included was a clothing and equipment list.

I was at home when the telegram came on June 26 with orders to report to the post office building in Buffalo for transportation to Fort Devens, Massachusetts. I was to report there on July 1 at 8:30 A.M. At that time there were four WAAC training centers: Fort Des Moines, Iowa; Fort Oglethorpe, Georgia; Daytona Beach, Florida; and Fort Devens, Massachusetts. I really wanted to go to Daytona Beach; I'd already visited Fort Devens. However, my disappointment was short-lived. The big adventure was beginning, and I was ready to go wherever fortune would take me.

My sisters Marie, Dot, and Anne drove Mom and me to the train station in Rochester. Anne had decided to come along with me and spend the night in Buffalo before I reported for induction. I was saddened at saying good-bye to the family, but having Anne along lessened the shock.

The next morning, I went over to the post office building, joined the inductees, and boarded the train. We stopped at Rochester to pick up another group, and to my surprise there was Laura Ehman, the home economics teacher from Friendship. We wound up in the same platoon of the same company.

In no time we were passing through Albany, then into Massachusetts and on to Worcester, where we left the train and boarded a bus for Ayer. It was a long ride at the 35 mph speed limit. At Ayer, two-and-a-half-ton army trucks picked us up and took us to the post. En route someone started singing "They say that in the army. . . . Yippee, I want to go home!" (That's the way it was sung at Fort Devens; at the other training centers it was "Gee, Mom, I wanna go home.") As we passed through the gates and drove to the WAAC area, some voices along the way called out of the darkness, "You'll be sorry!"—the traditional way of greeting inductees. The little pang of misgiving that struck me subsided as rapidly as it had come.

One

We were taken to the mess hall and given cocoa at 2:00 A.M. After someone showed us the proper way to make our army beds, we fell into them.

Three hours later, at 5:45 A.M., we were jolted with our first reveille. After breakfast we were marched off to take our advanced graduate certification test (AGCT). We were hardly in shape to have one little number determine whether or not we were "smart enough to be an officer," the goal of practically every recruit. I remember a black girl sitting near me who seemed to be having a terrible time with the test. Stressed as I was, I felt sorry for her.

At last came the long-awaited event, processing, when we would be given our uniforms. We were taken to a big quartermaster (QM) warehouse, where we lined up and recited our sizes as we passed by each place designated for a particular item. We were issued tan chino summer uniforms—a blouse (jacket), skirts, shirts of fine cotton, woolen ties, and OD (olive drab) jersey slips and strange panties, the crotches of which came nearly to the knees. We also received OD cotton stockings and woolen ankle socks but no bras. Somehow the army was never able to come to grips with the mind-boggling problems presented by our patriotic but oh-so-varied bosoms.

For fatigues we were given dresses of green and white pin-striped seersucker that buttoned down the front. *Fatigues* were exactly what the word implies. They were used for company details, the worst of which was KP.

Oxford shoes of rich brown leather, but otherwise plain and uninspiring, were issued for office work, social occasions, and dress formations. Civilian shoes were forbidden. We blanched when we saw the field shoes, called Li'l Abners. Like the oxfords, they were of high quality leather and made by Florsheim.

Our military wardrobe was completed with a light tannish green trench coat, a de Gaulle–style Hobby hat (named after Oveta Culp Hobby, director of the corps), chino overseas caps with pale yellow and light green piping (the corps colors), a shoulder handbag of brown coarse-grained leather, and smooth, soft leather gloves.

The handbags, which were lined with material that matched the trench coats, had places for everything, including a mirror. There was also a small change purse of the same color. At first the handbags were worn on the left shoulder, but later the order was changed and we had to wear them with the straps across our chests.

In the fall, after I went to Camp Carson, we were issued winter OD uniforms of fine wool, OD Hobby hats, and tapered overseas caps that fit the head snugly and looked much more attractive than the summer caps, which were like the men's. The winter overcoats were smart and military looking.

We were proud of our uniforms. Although they lacked the style and femininity of civilian clothing, uniforms were in vogue, and the materials were of high quality.

The major regulation of our personal appearance concerned our hair. Unlike men, who had to wear theirs clipped short, we could wear any hairstyle we could get under our hats, as long as our hair didn't touch our collar. Whenever a noncommissioned officer (NCO) had a particularly dirty job to be done, she would walk up and down the aisles during breakfast looking for wisps of hair hanging over collars. The guilty were dispatched to some ratty detail. There were no restrictions on the use of makeup and nail polish, which were important to women of the 1940s, as long as the effect wasn't "ostentatious."

Immediately after our arrival, we were issued a twenty-five-page memorandum that accounted for every possible contingency. Some of the more interesting ones included, under "Appearance": Large, unsightly combs will not be worn in the hair (as if it were possible to get them under the WAAC Hobby hat). "Gas Masks," under a special heading, decreed that "lipstick will be removed before using a gas mask." Another item, termed "Bedding," ordered that any evidence of bedbugs must be reported to the commander.

After processing, we settled down to the routines of basic training. I was assigned to Company 6 of the 31st Regiment along with several other ex-teachers, a contingent of loquacious southerners from upper Appalachia, some Pennsylvanians, and a motley group from the less affluent sections of metropolitan New York and New Jersey.

We occupied the usual two-story barracks in an older section of the post. Two rows of double bunks extended the length of the building. I was fortunate to have an upper. Recruits, not used to descending from such heights, were known to step on the face or other sensitive body parts of the person below.

I was always tired during "basic." I wasn't used to being thrown in with lots of people and having to get up early.

"Lights out" was at 10:00 or 10:30 P.M., but someone was always stirring around or calling back and forth after bed check. Two southerners, Luedell de Busk and Margaret Chittum, were particularly egregious offenders. One was at one end of the barracks and one at the other. They were great pals and had much of unimportance to say—all day long whenever possible—but after bedtime they were truly inspired. There were lapses, unfortunately, between conversations—just long enough for the rest of us to doze off while their thought processes were shifting into gear. Then "Chi-i-tum" or "de-ee-Busk!" We gave up shushing them because getting irritated made us more wide awake, and we were too tired to expend any more energy.

Our day began at 5:45 A.M. There'd be a rush to the mess hall for breakfast, only to find that the doors were still locked, necessitating our waiting outside while specks of soft coal soot from the mess hall fires drifted down on us. I still remember with nostalgia the smell of that soft coal dust. While waiting, we often sang a ditty to the tune of "The Old Gray Mare": "Here we stand like birds in the wilderness . . . waiting to be fed."

After breakfast we made our beds and got our areas in order in case inspections took place while we were having the usual round of training films, calisthenics, close-order drill, and classes.

I enjoyed the drilling and marching in formation, the army's pragmatic solution for moving great numbers of people and indoctrinating them to obey commands quickly—a primary necessity in combat situations. The part I liked most was marching to and from the barracks and classrooms. Someone in the rear would usually start to sing, and the platoon would pick it up. We learned a lot of songs concerned mainly with patriotism or the rigors of army life: "The

WAAC Is in Back of You," "They Say That in the Army," "I Wanna Go Home," "I've Got Sixpence," "It Was Bad when That Great Ship Went Down," the company song, et cetera. The one I liked the best, especially the last part, was sung to the tune of "Marching Along Together":

> We're khaki clad and we're mighty proud
> We're here to do our part
> Without a cannon, without a gun
> We'll do it with our hearts
> We are the WAAC, the army
> We're the W-A-A-C.

The songs were simple and the words trite, but we were caught up in the spirit of the times and none of that mattered. There was something almost mesmerizing when we marched and sang. The way I felt as the company moved in a unity of purpose and camaraderie was an emotional experience I never forgot.

The classes were interesting, but we were usually so tired that it was a struggle to keep awake. We studied map reading, chemical warfare, organization of the WAAC, safeguarding military information, military customs and courtesies, the Articles of War, and military sanitation. The military sanitation class was a prize. I don't think it had been altered since World War I. We took careful notes and even drew a diagram so we wouldn't make any mistakes and water our cavalry horses in the wrong section of a stream.

These classes were interspersed with training films, through which many of us slept when the lights were off. You had to watch it, though, because sometimes we'd be given a pop quiz. On the other hand, had we flunked, what could possibly have been done to us?

So we began to learn about the army and its methods of operation. In the barracks we practiced saluting and the about-face. In saluting it's important to keep the wrist from bending so that the arm is perfectly straight; at the same time it must be brought up snappily, with the forefinger a proper distance between the eyebrow and the hat, or cap. This provided a margin of about an inch. I got it down to perfection. West Point cadets couldn't surpass me.

The about-face is even more precise. The right toe must be placed behind the left heel, whereupon you pivot 180 degrees with the left heel and the right toe, arriving, you hope, in a sturdy, upright position facing the opposite direction. Even with practice you can wobble. We lived in dread of turning an ankle and falling flat, a mishap that would hardly lead to promotion.

I picked up army terminology quickly. However, I had one misunderstanding immediately after I arrived, when the sergeant yelled, "On the double!" Looking around for a partner, I asked some of the girls hurrying by if I could go with them, but they either ignored me or gave me a strange look. I was nearly late for formation.

I learned more from the varied types who made up the corps than I did in any of my courses. I had no idea of how sheltered my life had been until my contacts with factory girls from the big urban centers of the eastern seaboard. I remember my first experience on KP. A girl from New York's Lower East Side and I were detailed to clean the garbage cans. The army divided all disposable foodstuffs into two categories: edible, or soft garbage that could be consumed by animals, and inedible, which consisted of bones, melon rinds, eggshells, and coffee grounds. While we were engaged in scrubbing the cans, one of the cooks opened the back door, thrust a pan of garbage in my fellow sufferer's hands, and said, "Here, put this in the edible garbage." The girl looked a bit dazed, then said, "Edible! What's dat?" In my precise schoolteacher manner I explained that it meant it could be eaten. "Who'd wanna eat dis stuff?" she muttered as she headed for the "edible" can.

Advice passed along from an unknown source was that one should never volunteer. It was advice that I once, but only once, failed to follow. Helpers were needed at the men's officers' club, and I volunteered. Perhaps I thought some high brass would spot my exceptional abilities and recommend immediate promotion upon the completion of basic training. What those "officers and gentlemen" wanted were untiring cocktail waitresses. They were really putting away the drinks. I remember thinking how shocked my mother would be if she could witness that scene.

My upper bunk was no advantage the night about thirty of us suffered with diarrhea. There was a shortage of toilet paper and we were allowed only two squares per person. Toilets were continually flushing and the showers were busy. By the next morning, "troop movement" had taken on new meaning.

There wasn't much time for social and recreational activities. After I'd put in a day of tramping around in cotton stockings, woolen ankle socks, and a pair of Li'l Abners (it was an unusually hot, humid summer), I didn't feel like going any farther than the local PX. There I would buy a half pint of Sealtest orange sherbet and coffee ice cream and relish it on my way back to the barracks.

I did venture into Ayer a couple of times, to look at the shops and go to the military store, which had a marvelous collection of insignia and shoulder patches. I bought a couple of tiny bottles of liquor, which I took back to the post. Later, I had cause to regret this minor breach of regulations.

By early August basic was nearing completion and all kinds of LRs (latrine rumors) were circulating. The WAAC was to become the WAC (Women's Army Corps), a regular part of the army. This meant, for one thing, a different nomenclature in the ranking system. WAAC auxiliaries would be privates and first, second, and third officers would be captains, first, and second lieutenants, respectively. WAAC noncoms already had army equivalents.

What other changes would be made? Like most LRs, they would not be for the good. We learned that everyone would be discharged from the WAAC and would have to reenlist in the WAC. That meant a chance to get out by not reenlisting. What a tempting thought after the servitude of basic. Laura Ehman and I decided, half in tears, that we could never face people back home, especially after all the send-off parties and gifts. There was nothing to do but carry on. Besides, basic would be the worst, and we were looking forward to our first assignment. Most of us reenlisted.

There was only one week of basic left when we were marched to the post's huge parade ground for the swearing-in ceremony. We moved onto the field, formed the huge letters WAC (Company 6 of the 31st was down in the right foot of the A), and repeated the oath, company by company. It was all very exciting.

Tension mounted daily as orders began to come in. Besides assignments to various posts around the country, many would be sent to army schools for further training as secretaries, cooks, bakers, and auto mechanics. I prayed fervently that I wouldn't be sent to auto mechanics or cooks and bakers school. Those evenings when I'd gone to the PX, I'd seen the rough types who worked at motor transport—hardly choice companions or a choice army job. After my stint on KP, all I wanted to do in a mess hall was eat.

We waited. Every day more orders came in, and our ranks rapidly diminished. Mable Baker, a tall, thin, quiet girl from

Hollidaysburg, Pennsylvania, got her heart's desire—cooks and bakers. Maybe they'd passed up Brion. The barracks were closed and we were sent down to staging.

There wasn't much to do, which was a pleasant change. I went over to our orderly room (OR) in the old area where the furniture had been taken away and nothing was left except the guidon (banner) of Company 6. I was tempted to take it and was always sorry that I didn't.

We were sitting around in the barracks one day when suddenly we were ordered to fall out, dressed as we were and without our purses. A theft had been reported and a search would be conducted of all our belongings. I remembered the little bottles of liquor I'd bought in Ayer and stashed in my barracks bag in anticipation of a train journey. I sweated. We were finally dismissed, and I hurried in. My things had not been searched. I grabbed the bottles, rushed to the latrine, and flushed the contents down the toilet. A number of other toilets were flushing simultaneously.

We still waited for orders. A group was sent to Daytona Beach. Then at last we were called out, and the names of a dozen of us, all ex-teachers and close friends by now, were read. We were ordered to Camp Carson, Colorado, to form a new detachment. Daytona no longer mattered. I was going west, to the Rockies, and I knew it was going to be a beautiful place.

On August 19, 1943, we rode out of Fort Devens for the last time. The highlight of my trip west was my first glimpse of the prairie in Nebraska, with scattered windmills and grazing white-faced cattle. Miles and miles on the train, clickety-clack, clickety-clack, and then, on the horizon, the purple-gray outline of the Rockies. I was indescribably thrilled.

Two

We arrived at Camp Carson, at the base of Cheyenne Mountain, and were greeted by our new CO, Lieutenant Lillian Mazzei, and 1st Sgt. Ysleta B. Harlee. Except for the cooks and the company clerk, we were the first Wacs at Camp Carson. Lieutenant Mazzei gave us the usual pep talk, emphasizing the importance of the WAC image for which we'd be responsible and stating firmly there'd be no "tramps" in her company. She told us we were lucky to be in the nicest camp in the country, and if she ever got any reports of bad conduct, we'd see the miscreant's bags by the orderly room door, awaiting immediate departure. This CO obviously was going to be strictly GI. It was evident from our first glimpse of Sergeant Harlee, who had an eye like an unpredictable horse, that she'd never brook any tomfoolery either.

On my first day at Camp Carson I found myself elbow deep in suds among the pots and pans, looking through a window with a marvelous view of Cheyenne Mountain. I was euphoric.

However, the euphoria vanished rapidly the next day when we were all put on what the army calls a "shit detail."

It was literally that. One of the company's NCOs had a little dog she kept in the empty barracks that was to become our new home. Our job was to clean up its past calls of nature. We squeamishly attended to our task, after which we washed windows. Welcome to Camp Carson.

As new arrivals came from other training commands and posts, most were assigned to jobs immediately. Although it was exciting to size them up as they arrived, we anxiously waited for our assignments. Meanwhile, we were doing whatever details Lieutenant Mazzei and Sergeant Harlee could dream up. When they ran short of inspiration, they'd have us police the area (passersby, visitors, and dates were inconsiderate about GI'ing their cigarette butts). The army didn't want anyone to have an unoccupied moment lest she enjoy some relaxation, cause trouble, or have a nervous breakdown and require a Section 8.

I really enjoyed one of the details and would have been content to have it for my regular assignment. It required wheeling, with help, a large barrowlike vehicle to the QM area to pick up supplies and bring them back to the detachment. While waiting I could chat with the GIs who located the supplies, checked them off the lists, and helped with the loading. The weather was dry, sunny, and invigorating, and I could look up at the mountains as I huffed and puffed my way home.

One day Lieutenant Mazzei called me in and said, "Brion, I understand that you like to paint. They're working on a big musical down at the theater and they need someone to do some painting. Would you be interested?"

"Oh, yes, ma'am," I said, conjuring up the excitement of painting stage scenery while actors and musicians scurried about and technicians tried to keep pace with demands for moving props and adjusting lights. Or I might be called on to stand in for some flubbing actress and my considerable dramatic abilities could be put to use. I was most pleased.

When I reported to the theater, I was given a pair of coveralls and a long piece of rope to tie around my waist to keep them up so I wouldn't trip (I was skinny and the overalls were large). Then, with a bucket of light blue paint and a male corporal to move the ladder, I was put to work painting one wall of the theater. He would sit down in one of the theater seats while I painted as far as I could reach, at which point I'd come down the ladder and he'd move it and sit down again. I didn't get even a glimpse of any dramatic activities all day long. I was exhausted when I got back to the barracks, but I went off dutifully the next day. The morning wore on and finally it was time for lunch.

I'd had it, so I went in to brave Lieutenant Mazzei and request to be taken off the detail. There were tears in my eyes. She was angry, as I'd feared (we'd already discovered her hot temper), but not for the reason I'd thought. "Nobody," she said, "is going to exploit my girls." She told me not to go back, dismissed me, and got on the phone. That was the end of that.

The musical was *Strictly GI,* an all-soldiers revue with original music, a cast of fifty soldiers and Wacs, and the 89th Division Artillery Band. The big show was good. When I attended with friends, I pointed out my artistic contribution. In fact, every time I went to the theater after that, I always took a look at that wall.

By now everyone in our group had been assigned to offices except five of us who couldn't type. We lived in dread of being sent to the hospital detachment, where there'd be an endless round of carrying bedpans, mopping floors, carrying food trays, and making beds. By comparison, motor transport and cooks and bakers looked idyllic. However, we were packed off to a dental clinic, where the most attractive one of us went to work keeping dental records and the rest of us became dental assistants.

The mental skills required by my job were hardly taxing. With an air hose in one hand and a water hose in the other, I'd stand and wait while the dentist was drilling. When he'd pause, I'd spray the GI's mouth with water, the GI would spit, I'd give the tooth a little blast of air, and the dentist would go to work again with the drill. When he was satisfied, he'd have me mix a filling and hand him the necessary instruments and devices while he put it in. Afterward, I would sterilize whatever could be put in the sterilizer, wipe off everything else with alcohol, and record the nature of the work done on each patient.

Not only did I hate my work but I was being deprived of wearing my uniform, a vital part of being in the army. The first few days we wore white hospital gowns over our shirts and skirts, but the women civilians who worked there objected to our wearing the same thing they did. It was obvious that they considered us inferior. Instead of the gowns, we were forced to wear a ghastly medium-blue seersucker dress like the hospital attendants wore. The dresses made us look round shouldered and wide hipped. We despised them.

Besides my fellow Wacs, the people with whom I was most closely associated at the dental clinic were Lt. Col. Glenn Chaffee, from Arkansas, a dear monkey-faced man who was the chief; 1st Lt. Lawrence J. Jones, of Columbus, Ohio, with whom I worked the longest; and Lt. Paul Sweeney, of Pittsburgh, Jones's replacement when he was transferred to Hawaii.

Lieutenant Jones was fortyish, with graying temples, and wasn't especially handsome, but he had a quiet, gentle manner that was quite sexy. I developed a crush on him after he removed one of my bicuspids. I was desolate when he left, but Lieutenant Sweeney proved to be a splendid antidote. He was a pudgy fellow with a slightly pockmarked face, a naughty eye, and a ready wit. He livened up my job and relieved the apprehension of his patients, with whom we joked freely.

Of the enlisted men who worked at the clinic, my favorite was Hiram Hollingsworth, a big, heavy fellow with a gold tooth that flashed when he laughed, which was frequently. The cause of his mirth was usually a ditty that he sang that was appropriate to the daily activities at the clinic:

> *Down at the zoo they all ask for you*
> *They all ask for you. Yes, they all ask for you*
> *Down at the zoo they all ask for you*
> *Oh, the monkeys ask and the camels ask and*
>   *the . . . .*
> *They all ask for you.*

Besides my friends, most of whom lived with me on the second floor of barrack 1642, there were Lieutenant Mazzei and our company NCOs. Lieutenant Mazzei had worked in a bank in Newark, New Jersey, before entering the corps. She was of Sicilian-Italian ancestry, with dark hair and penetrating black eyes that took you apart in little pieces, put you together again, and left you doubting whether or not you met with her approval. The severity of her expression was enhanced by a light scar that ran down one cheek. Underneath this rather formidable exterior was a good person, and I respected her.

First Sergeant Harlee was a West Texan and rough around the edges. Although her tolerance threshold was low, she was kind and forthright, and I quickly became fond of her.

I came to her special attention when she discovered that Scotty Martin, whom I was dating, was in her boyfriend's company, the 315th Engineers of the 89th Division. He was Scotty's first sergeant. After that I always got a "Hi, Brion" and a warm smile. Unlike the sort of thing one expected from a top sarge, she once left me a note that read: Brion, you have CQ Sunday. If you have a heavy date, see me.

The supply sergeant T4g. was Gracie Hines. She wore a blandly prim expression and a pair of glasses that slipped down to the end of her nose. Gracie knew every article of clothing you had, how long you'd had it, and whether or not you needed it in the next six months. She meant business. Later, Gracie was to fall from favor. Sergeant Harlee told me that Lieutenant Mazzei was thinking of transferring her and offering me the job. I would have made staff sergeant, but the army was to intervene with a better deal.

Corporal Evelyn Javaris, a Greek girl with a pleasant round face, was our baker. I endeared myself to her and the cook, Rose, by my constant requests for seconds. As a result, I was usually given the less disagreeable tasks when I got KP, things like cleaning the tables in the dining room and lining up the salt and pepper shakers and the sugar bowls.

Because the army tends to weld a disparate group of people living closely together into a unity, my friends were those who lived in the barracks with me. Besides the experiences we shared, most of us had a lot in common. We were fairly well educated, motivated to help the war effort, even if we had jobs that weren't challenging, and sympathetic to one another's needs. There was little, if any, hostility when promotions came through for some and not others. My group of friends consisted of Evelyn Searls, a cheerful, intelligent, and academically well-informed girl from Redlands, California, who had a delightful chuckle and never complained when given a disagreeable task; Loretta Townsend, slightly reserved but warmly sympathetic and responsive to humorous situations; Emmeline Riley, exceptionally witty with a marvelous sense of the ridiculous, and uniquely innovative in altering song lyrics to fit WAC predicaments; Alice Dixon, a good-natured tease who had taught in the public schools of upstate New York; and Eleanor Sneed, of Charleroi, Pennsylvania, pretty, tall, and slender, griping halfheartedly as she went about her barracks duties. Eleanor was both witty and adventuresome.

One day a new member was added to the list. The front door opened with a flourish and there stood an attractive bleached blonde. She surveyed us with a slightly contemptuous look and announced flatly that she was Mary Ann Reed. This implied a person of importance. I held my breath because the cot next to mine was vacant and I was afraid it was destined for her. It was. She plunked down an expensive leather suitcase, turned to me, and said, "Who are *you?*" It was obvious that I was someone insignificant. All barracks activity had ceased. She proceeded to unpack with interspersed comments about the army's stupidity and hers for having joined it. We were aghast. She could never be one of *us*. If she read our minds, which she probably did, she didn't appear to care.

Mary Ann loved to shock. Her uncanny knowledge of human frailties enabled her to hit her target dead center. When she discovered that most of us had been teachers, she had a heyday. However, her remarks were for a general audience, which she had no difficulty in finding. She sensed immediately that I was more fascinated than shocked, so she abandoned that approach with me and decided to take me under her wing and teach me a thing or two. "You're such a babe in the woods," she'd tell me. "You don't know anything about the *real* world." "You're so dumb it's painful." And so on. She told me she'd been a chorus girl, and she seemed knowledgeable about a side of life that was unfamiliar to me. I wanted to learn about life, and I knew I'd found the right teacher.

Mary Ann was assigned to the dental clinic, where she created her usual sensation. Colonel Chaffee introduced her to all of us, then took her over to one of the officers who needed an assistant. Although dentistry was new to her, it was difficult to tell who was assisting whom. The other men stole quick, envious looks.

One afternoon while we were waiting to go to the mess hall, she looked at me with apparent disgust and said, "Brion, doesn't anyone ever feed you? You're so *skinny*. One good fart and you'd be halfway to the moon. Of course it's no wonder with the damn crap the army dishes out. Tomorrow night I'm taking you into town and we're having a decent steak dinner, big, thick, and juicy. And no cheap joint, either. When I do a thing, I do it *right*, and since you're so shit-poor I'm footing the bill."

The next night as we headed for the orderly room to sign out, I remarked that we'd have to hurry to get in line for the bus. "Bus!" she exploded scornfully. "A bus!" She wrinkled her nose with disgust and curled her lip in her characteristic way. "We're going in a taxi, kid. When you go somewhere with me, you go in style." So we went to Colorado Springs in a taxi and had a terrific meal at the Village Inn, where enlisted personnel were permitted to go. Mary Ann showed her expertise with the wine and had the waiters scurrying to please her.

Some of my less perceptive friends wondered why I put up with her belittling remarks, but it wasn't long before she was wholeheartedly accepted by all and admired for her absolute honesty and spunk. Everyone enjoyed the way she livened things up with her unpredictable, incisive comments. Even her spicy language no longer seemed objectionable. Strangely, she used it in a way that was both ladylike and in keeping with her salty character.

The cot on the other side of Mary Ann's belonged to Virgie Kamil, who often slept on her back with her eyes open. Mary Ann said it gave her the creeps because she looked like a "damn corpse" and kept her awake thinking of it lying next to her. Virgie was one of those people who were annoying, not by doing but just by being. It wasn't her looks, although she had bulging gray eyes, wore glasses, and was pudgy. She never seemed to say anything of note. In fact, she never seemed to say anything. I couldn't define what about her put people off. However, there was one occasion when she provided a clue. It stirred up a proverbial hornet's nest.

Saturday morning's formal inspections interfered with Friday night's social life because we couldn't go out until we had our area dusted and cleaned and all our belongings in the prescribed places in our footlocker and closet. Cleaning meant light mopping our area. All clothes hanging in our closet had to face the designated direction with all buttons buttoned. Shoes had to be lined up with the toes along a certain edge of a floorboard. They had to be tied in one loop with the laces tucked in. Virgie zealously put bleach in her mop water, with the result that her patch of floor stood out and made the rest of ours look dirty. We all got gigged (received demerits) and were confined to the area—on a Saturday night. Not only that, but Virgie used so much water that it seeped through the cracks of the floor and dripped on people below. With murder in their hearts, a delegation confronted us. Virgie was blandly impassive. There was nothing to do but wait for the drips to cease and the delegation's wrath to subside.

Inspections required careful attention to details at all times. Spot checks could occur while we were away at work, just to keep us on our toes. Chiefly, they were to see that beds were properly made, the latrines were clean, and the day room (recreation room) was in order. Blankets had to be tucked tightly enough so a penny would bounce, and exactly six inches of the upper sheet had to be folded over the blanket. (To be assured of this, a GI toothbrush could be used as a ruler.) The pillow would then be covered with a second blanket folded in half and precisely tucked over the top part of the cot. To check this, a bed was picked at random, usually one that looked suspicious, and the inspector ripped off the top blanket and looked under the pillow. If it didn't pass, the owner of the bed was gigged.

Besides making our beds before leaving for work, we usually had to serve on a latrine or day room squad, each of which had a person in charge to see that everything was in order. In charge of the latrine squad was the "latrine queen," who didn't dare leave until the rest had gone for fear there'd be lipstick or hair in the sinks or blobs of toothpaste on the faucets. She took the rap for everything neglected. I got gigged once because a speck of toothpaste was found on one of the faucets.

Once Lieutenant Mazzei gigged the lot of us and confined us to the barracks. Ruth Shaver's father was passing through Colorado Springs on his way to the West Coast. Ruth and he had planned to meet briefly, but Lieutenant Mazzei refused Ruth's request for a postponement of a detention. No doubt her long record of gigs for a sloppy bed clinched the decision. Ruth missed seeing her father. Everyone was enraged, but after our fury subsided we referred to her as "the girl who got so many gigs that nothing could save her." Ruth eventually was transferred to New Mexico. When we received letters from her, which were heavily censored, Evelyn Searls remarked, "Isn't it just like the army to be guarding sand in barren New Mexico?" Her letters came from a place called Los Alamos.

An embarrassing situation resulted from an incident that occurred when I was on a squad cleaning the day room. Mary Ann was on the same detail, doing the dusting. As we were finishing, she flicked the dust cloth in my face and ran out, closing the door with me in hot pursuit. I didn't notice that the door was still in motion, and I hit the edge of it dead center down the front of my body. I was thrown backward, but with no damage except bruises, which appeared the next day. As luck would have it, we were being given our monthly pelvic examination. (Army regulations required the male equivalent, so this was what they came up with for us. Fortunately, someone in the higher WAC echelons soon had it quashed.) Of course the "peek and poke" captain saw the bruises and inquired as to their cause. What could I say, I ran into a door? But I had, so I said it. No doubt his worst opinions of Wacs were confirmed.

In addition to our jobs and barrack duties, other things cut into our time. One of these was physical training, which we did every day when we first got up. We were awakened by a whistle, not a bugle, and the lights were turned on. We rolled out and did a set of exercises in our pajamas, beside our beds—not enthusiastically or vigorously, but enough to satisfy regulations. We also had drill in the field outside our mess hall. I remember being taken out shortly after the company was complete and before we were used to marching together. Gracie Sigelman and the other short ones in the rear were having a hard time keeping up, and all of us were bobbing up and down and stumbling over stones and holes in the uneven terrain. Sergeant Harlee was losing control of both us and herself and was shrieking that we looked worse than a herd of Rocky Mountain billy goats. Everyone was upset because we wanted to make a good impression at "retreat."

The weekly retreat, at sunset, always thrilled me. One by one the units on the post marched onto the parade ground. As the bugler blew the stirring call, the flag was slowly lowered. The notes were like crystals on the crisp air, and the sky glowed a pale red behind the snowy peaks of the mountains. Those were moments when I felt the greatest pride in our country and the role that each person standing so quietly was playing in this latest great episode in human history.

The deeply moving experience of the retreat not only enhanced my patriotism, it intensified my love for the new state in which I had been located. From the first moment of my arrival, I had been enchanted with Colorado—the towering mountains that rose so unexpectedly from the expanse of dry, flat plain; the impenetrable blueness of the sky; and the air, indescribably invigorating, so unlike that in the humid climate I had always known. Like Brigham Young as he first viewed the valley around the Great Salt Lake, I knew I'd found "The Place."

I welcomed the opportunity to be out of doors, even though it often meant drilling with the company after working all day. We had to keep up our marching skills for retreat and possible public appearance if called upon to do so.

The detachment took part in two parades in Colorado Springs. The first was at Thanksgiving. Because we were marching before civilians for the first time, we were eager to do better than the men, and everyone was tense, especially Lieutenant Mazzei and the NCOs. Three two-and-a-half-ton trucks were brought in to take us into town, and one of the NCOs was shrieking frantically, trying to get us loaded. We were dressed in our OD best, and the skirts were impeding our climbing aboard. We had to put one foot into one of the iron loops on the tailgate and swing the other leg up to the truck bed. Because the loop was at least three feet from the ground, the short-legged girls had to be boosted. Another NCO kept screeching "On the double!" and everyone at the rear of the trucks was getting bunched up like a flock of sheep. We were frustrated and resentful of the way it was handled.

We were finally loaded. As we started to pull away, I made a baaing noise, which was picked up rapidly. We rolled down F Street, bleating and baaing. Despite the humiliating take-off and the high school band that played too fast for the army stride, we did beautifully. It was important to make a good showing because this was the first time that most of us paraded before civilians.

The other parade, to celebrate the second anniversary of the WAAC-WAC, was held on Memorial Day and went off without incident. We finally received some tangible recognition when our photograph was published in the Colorado Springs newspaper.

There were plenty of things to do when we weren't working. First on the list was dating. It often proved disappointing, because we weren't allowed to date officers, and it always seemed that the nicest enlisted men were either transferred or sent off for combat. However, that never seemed to stop us. We had to be in by 11:00 P.M. except on Saturday, when we could stay out until 2:00 A.M.

During the week we'd spend a lot of time at the PX, having Cokes and milk shakes, chatting, and watching the action while the jukebox belted out the old favorites: "Pistol Packin' Mama," "Don't Fence Me In," "Paper Doll," "I'll Be Around," and "I'll Get By."

Besides the PX, there was the 7th Service Command NCO Club, which served liquor and wasn't as crowded. I don't recall any rowdiness there. It was mainly a place to go and have fun talking, dancing to the jukebox, and drinking after an arduous day. One evening Evelyn, Loretta, and I were invited to go with her boss, Sgt. Bob Elder. We were hardly the types to go astray, but we did. Our undoing was tequila, which we drank for the first time in a mixed drink that tasted deceptively mild. Suddenly we decided we'd better head back to the detachment, a fair distance that we had to negotiate on foot. Apparently we decided to take a shortcut across the muddy lot beside the orderly room on our way to sign in.

When I awoke the next day, all of my clothes were neatly folded, muddy shoes lined up under the bed, and my uniform facing the proper direction with the buttons buttoned as for Saturday morning inspection. All looked well until I went out to breakfast and saw the evidence of our folly—zigzagging footprints preserved for posterity by an overnight freeze.

It was fun to go into Colorado Springs and have cocktails and dinner at one of the good restaurants, such as the Blue Spruce, the Village Inn, or the Copper Grove of the Antlers Hotel. At first the best places would admit only civilians and officers, but word apparently got to the right authorities and the ban against enlisted personnel was lifted. With that barrier removed, some of us splurged and went to the Broadmoor. It was wild and alive with officers of higher ranks. One particular major would stagger to our table, lean over it, look at us with bleary eyes, and then wander off. On one of these occasions he left his cap. I lifted his oak leaf, which I took back to the barracks and wore on my pajamas.

Various outfits on the post gave dances, to which we were invited: the MPs, a QM truck unit, the 3d Battalion of the

201st Infantry. The best, given by the 413th Mule Pack Artillery of the 104th Timberwolf Division, was held in the Elks Club ballroom in Colorado Springs rather than on the post like most of the others. It's likely that some of the fellows I danced with that night were killed when the 104th crossed the Rhine at Remagen, Germany.

Some of the outfits gave variety shows and other presentations, which we attended. Scotty Martin took me to a show called "Veterinary Varieties," given by the 30th Veterinary Hospital. The program, consisting mainly of songs and skits, included a trio of blackface, antics in a loan office, misadventures in a station hospital ward, and comic episodes in a bookie office. It was funny and the music was good. Scotty, whom I dated until the 89th Division was whisked away to Europe, was about my height and slightly stocky, with wavy dark blond hair and blue eyes. His greatest assets were his sense of humor and a fine tenor voice. That evening we really clicked, especially when it came to singing. We sang all the way home.

The WAC gave a show of its own, for the American Legion in Colorado Springs. Mainly for public relations purposes, we slipped in a few items that we hoped would counteract the undeserved image of the corps—for instance, the fact that approximately half of the company qualified for officer candidate school and a third were college educated, 10 percent of those having done graduate work or earned a master's degree. The skit showed how the army took in a heterogeneous group of women and converted them into "beautiful, streamlined, charming, capable Wacs." Knowing the American Legion, it probably fell on deaf ears, but we tried.

It was always a struggle to have any kind of intellectual life, but we managed to take advantage of whatever was available. The library for our part of the post, located in the PX, was geared for light, entertaining reading, but if we looked carefully, we could find a few biographies and other nonfiction that was both readable and informative. The books were mostly donations. The library was a welcome and tranquil refuge during the winter when the chinook was blowing or when the barracks were too noisy for reading. Some interesting men went there, including many ex-ASTPs (army specialized training program); in typical army fashion, they had been dumped into the infantry regiments of the 104th Division. (Spiteful army brass, I presume, had protested their being kept stateside for college training.) We had some good exchanges about the books we were reading.

The Colorado Springs Fine Arts Center and Colorado College provided opportunities for concerts and art exhibits. I saw "Martha" and "The Marriage of Figaro," both presented by the music department of Colorado College. Another highlight was a concert given by Vivian della Chiesa, a popular opera star whom my mother particularly loved.

Trips into Colorado Springs were time-consuming. By the time we walked home from work, showered and dressed, and waited in a long bus line (taxis were busy and too expensive for the lower enlisted ranks), it was getting late. After a half-hour ride into town and further waiting in the crowded restaurants, there was little time to go to a movie, concert, or library before we had to return to the camp. Consequently, we postponed these activities until the weekend.

At first we were annoyed that our next-door neighbors, the conscientious objectors, had so much free time and ready access to the town. They were a motley collection that included numerous foreigners, obvious from brief conversations and hearing their names called at mail call. The army had put them into a single unit and quartered them next to us, away from all the other outfits on the post, at the eastern edge of the camp. Many appeared to be unassigned, and transfers in and out were frequent. Eventually, we learned from Ruth Shaver, who worked for the provost marshal, that passes to Colorado Springs and Denver were issued freely in order to determine the contacts of several who were involved in an extensive German espionage ring. Army intelligence broke up the ring and transferred the conscientious objectors elsewhere.

As the holiday season approached, we were busy preparing programs, first for Thanksgiving and then for our first army Christmas. I was mistress of ceremonies for Thanksgiving. An organist, Letha Royce, played one of the army's portable organs for the musical selections. Then Leora Weimar gave the blessing, after which everyone sang WAC songs, followed by a Thanksgiving reading and two solos by Lieutenant Mazzei.

Those of us who enjoyed singing practiced carols for the Christmas program. Lieutenant Mazzei sang "Jesu Bambino" in her rich contralto voice with a chorus of us singing the accompanying parts. It was moving and nostalgic and inspired a feeling of closeness. I wondered where we'd be the next Christmas.

Thinking of the Christmas festivities going on at home dampened my spirits, but I was heartened by the prospect of my upcoming furlough. Theoretically, we were eligible for one after six months of service and one for each six months thereafter. Many of us, having come straight from basic, were entitled to one at the same time, so each had to wait her turn so that office work forces would not be depleted. My turn came in early January.

On January 14, I left on the *Rocky Mountain Rocket,* the Rock Island's express train to Chicago, where I had to change to another line for Rochester. The train was crowded, and soot drifted in. Betty Hooverman, who also had a furlough, was with me, and we passed the long overnight ride chatting with GIs and trying to keep warm without using our blouses or overcoats. We'd brought hangers for them so we could arrive home looking smart and unwrinkled. I got into Rochester the next evening, suddenly perky despite the thirty-hour trip. Marie and Mom met me at the station.

I went to East Rochester to see Aunt Alice Hieber, and Mom took me to church to show me off in my uniform. Bill and Elsie came home, and someone took a picture of the whole family. It would be the last time we'd all be together.

Shortly before I got back to Colorado, it was Mary Ann's turn to go home. The girls said she'd been bragging about how she was going to "kick the army's backside and get the hell out of here and go back to civilization and *live*." Although she supposedly was from Elgin, Texas, she went to Lakewood, Ohio. While she was gone I received a penny postcard:

> Hello Birdlegs,
> I hope you put on a little more meat while you were away. It's been a long time since I've argued with you. All in all you're a good kid. And don't forget to dust under my bed. We sure had a time while you kids were gone. Some fun. But will be glad to get back.
> Love,
> Mary Ann

One afternoon shortly after I received the card, the barracks door was flung open and there stood Mary Ann. Someone said, "Well look who's back already, a week before her furlough's over!"

"Yaah, I missed you creeps. Besides, it was dead back there," she remarked disgustedly.

We had to rub it in, but she could tell that everyone was glad to see her. She was gruffly pleased.

February 2, 1944, was a red-letter day. At last I was promoted to private first class. I raced off to get the stripes right away and diligently sewed them on everything. I was a private first class for twenty-seven days. On March 1, I became a technician, fifth grade—in short, a corporal. At this rate, I thought, there was no telling how high I was going to go. Well, it turned out that it wasn't going to be far. Ratings were frozen, and a thaw, at least for me, never occurred.

I always thought I got my stripes by being mistress of ceremonies for a program that we presented for a visiting WAC major from Des Moines. The major was impressed with the songs and the way the program was put together. Undoubtedly it made points for Lieutenant Mazzei, perhaps making her decide to take another look at Brion.

The promotion didn't increase my pay significantly. As a private I received fifty dollars a month, which was raised to fifty-four dollars when I became a private first class. When I was promoted to corporal, it rose to sixty-six dollars, hardly a windfall, but the army provided nearly everything we needed so money wasn't important. What made it a big deal was that I no longer had to do KP.

To celebrate my farewell to that onerous duty, and simultaneously reward the remaining unfortunates for whom I felt a surge of pity, I sketched a design for a badge, which they deserved. Inspired by a badge given to infantrymen for marksmanship, it had corresponding appendages for those qualifying as experts in the most odious KP chores: pots and pans, garbage, and grease trap.

In place of KP, we were assigned to charge of quarters (CQ) duties. The CQ presided at the first sergeant's desk during off-duty hours. Her tasks included answering the telephone, taking messages, keeping track of people signing in and out, and handling any emergency that might arise.

Unfortunately, an emergency arose my first night on CQ. A wealthy lady from Colorado Springs, doing her bit for the war, gave the WAC detachment one of her pedigreed dogs for a mascot. It was a large, streamlined, short-haired creature with pale, woebegone, reproachful eyes and a skinny tail. Not knowing what to do with it, Sergeant Harlee had it put in an empty room off the orderly room. Only a thin wall separated the two rooms. Lieutenant Mazzei was working late in her office and waiting for her date to pick her up. When I announced his arrival she came out, and they stood talking for a few moments. His back was to me, but I could see Lieutenant Mazzei's face over his shoulder. Suddenly there was a commotion in the other room. Burbling and explosive defecating sounds were bouncing off the walls. Lieutenant Mazzei was having difficulty keeping her composure while continuing the conversation, motioning to me to take action and maneuvering her date to the door. They exited. When I looked in on the scene, there stood the dog, spent from his ordeal, the room festooned with his contributions. Knowing Sergeant Harlee's short fuse, I left her a carefully written note. The Augean task was probably assigned to Gracie Hines the next morning, and by afternoon we were minus a mascot.

We had one other mascot before this, an adorable black spaniel puppy named Tiny Wac. She used to run along beside us as we marched to retreat. When promotions came through, she became a private first class and wore her stripe on a little OD coat. She, too, wasn't with us very long.

One day a transfer arrived, a sort of bewildered derelict who was virtually mentally retarded. The army supposedly rejected the slow witted, but there were numerous occasions when we didn't believe it. This was one of those occasions. Lieutenant Mazzei and Sergeant Harlee didn't know what to do with her, so they put her in the supply room to help Gracie Hines. It wasn't working out, but she stayed there until the day she committed a grievous error. Sergeant Harlee's boyfriend sent her a dozen long-stemmed roses, which were handed to the woman to put in a vase. When she came back, the stems had been cut short and the roses were flopping in all directions in a bowl. "Well, it said 'cut flowers'" was all she could offer by way of explanation. She was off to the hospital detachment the following day.

At about this time public relations (PR) descended on the dental clinic as part of a scheme to show the variety of ways that Wacs were doing their patriotic duty. Enlistments were dwindling, and something short of a draft was needed. (Actually a draft was under serious consideration.) Public reltions arrived with a signal corps photographer to take pictures to send back to our home newspapers.

The dental officers seemed powerless to quell Mary Ann's caustic comments. They hoped to shut her up by having her pose while assisting Captain Watson, thought to be a quieting influence. But Captain Watson had a "lazy eye" that shifted to the outside corner at unexpected moments. One last remark Mary Ann couldn't resist making prompted his eye to stray just as the camera flashed. It's doubtful if the scene ever spurred enlistment.

The cameraman took a picture of me with Captain Dickey. I didn't want to be photographed in one of those god-awful blue gowns and have it sent to a newspaper back home. Meanwhile, Mary Ann had taken one of the PR men aside and was filling him in on office details. She was quite pleased with herself. On the way home she sang her favorite ditty:

> *If I were as low as a morsel of snow*
> *I'd look up at you and go: Plpppppp [raspberry]*
> *If I were as high as a bird in the sky*
> *I'd look down on you and go: Plpppppp. . . .*

It was a perfect expression of her feelings about the military and her general attitude toward life.

During that winter, my life at Camp Carson hummed along in its usual way: hundreds of teeth drilled and plugged, dates of no special interest who came and went, and several parties, dances, and forays to the service club. Roxy Reppond was called for overseas duty. How we envied her. We gave her a big dinner party in Colorado Springs. Then I received a postcard from my sister Anne:

> Dear Ren,
> Had my physical and have been accepted into the Air WAC. Isn't it great!
> Al is flying home—should arrive Sat. or Sun.
> Called me four times. I can hardly wait.
> Will write a letter later on and give all the details. Had my physical in Buffalo. 12 of us went up on the train. 9 of us passed. Write soon.
> Love,
> Sis

One weekend Mary Ann and Janie Laulette went horseback riding in the Garden of the Gods, at that time an untouched area with unusual red rock formations outside of Colorado Springs. Janie returned bruised. All we got out of

Mary Ann, who was a little the worse for wear herself, was that "a jockey couldn't ride those damn nags!" Janie merely commented that she had a "lousy headache." But we had the picture. She had imbibed too much, and Mary Ann, who seldom drank and never dated, was apparently carried away by an extra cocktail, the altitude, and the horse.

By this time a holiday was in order. Evelyn Searls, Alice Dixon, and I got overnight passes and went to Denver. That evening we had dinner at a lovely hotel. There was the usual wartime line waiting for tables. The maitre d' appeared and said he had a table for four. An older lady who was standing in front of me suggested we might share it. We agreed. Looking distastefully at us, the maitre d' called to the young man who was escorting people to their tables and said, "Table for one *lady* and three *Wacs*." The incident cast a pall over the dinner we'd so eagerly awaited. Although humiliations of that sort were to occur many times, I never learned to brush them off.

Unknown to us, the War Department was aware of vicious rumors that were circulating about the loose morals of the WAC, seriously curtailing enlistment. Suspecting that the Axis may have instigated a campaign to discourage the enlistment of an anticipated million women who would release men for combat, the department began an exhaustive investigation. Military intelligence, with the cooperation of the Federal Bureau of Investigation (FBI), began tracing the origin of the most virulent rumors. After months of interviews with hundreds of people from all sections of the country, but especially the eastern seaboard, where the slander was most extensive, the evidence indicated that the obscene rumors resulted not from Nazi propaganda but from servicemen themselves. The men, who resented and feared replacement by women, fabricated stories or embellished hearsay, which they passed along to their relatives, wives, and girlfriends. Ultimately the fabrications reached the whole population. Credence was lent to the rumors by the thousands of civilian women in near-military uniforms whose public behavior was not subject to the twenty-four-hour-a-day restriction of Wacs. (These quasi-WAC uniforms, often made of the same WAC cotton and OD materials, could be purchased in clothing stores across the country.) Male chauvinists and other bigoted people seized any excuse to denigrate women who they thought were competing with men.

One day Mary Ann announced that she was going to Colorado Springs to get her hair dyed. "None of those cheap dye jobs," she said, disdainfully. This one was being done in the "ritziest salon in the whole damn town," and when she did a thing she didn't "skimp," et cetera. Mary Ann, who had been a bleached blonde, came back a brunette.

She couldn't wait to put in her appearance at the dental clinic the next morning, and neither could I. We set off a little later than usual, so most of the officers would be there. Colonel Chaffee met us at the door, his monkey face beaming. Then he paused for a moment and exclaimed, "Why Private Reed, a blonde yesterday and a brunette today." "Hell, yes," she said, breezing past him, "and I might be a redhead tomorrow."

Spring came, green and glorious. The snow melted from the mountainsides, and the fields beside our barracks acquired a scattering of flowers. Coming home one day we passed a guard accompanying three German prisoners of war (POWs) who were picking flowers and exclaiming delightedly over their finds. Was there a war going on?

The POWs had a camp near the post, on the main road to Colorado Springs, and we used to see them outdoors in the midst of winter, playing volleyball, torsos bare and wearing shorts. When the Barnum & Bailey circus came that spring, the Germans were marched out of their compound, past our barracks, and through the camp to the grounds where the circus was set up. Nothing like entertainment for the enemy. We weren't given the same opportunity.

It was against army regulations to photograph POWs but the temptation was so great that Eleanor Sneed took a few pictures. But who would develop them? We didn't dare have it done through the PX, so we took them to a civilian shop in town. We were nervous for fear the shop would notice what we'd taken and report us. Nothing happened. The pictures turned out fine except that our subjects were too far away to show the precision with which they marched.

The last few months before my transfer from Camp Carson were tranquil, especially after the departure of the 104th. I felt at home in the detachment, at the dental clinic, and on the post itself. I was happy to stay put if I couldn't have an overseas assignment.

There was an empty room at the end of our floor of the barracks that normally would have been used by company noncoms. Our NCOs bunked elsewhere. Lieutenant Mazzei gave us permission to make the room into a lounge. Someone acquired chairs, Gracie Hines let us have a cot, which we decorated with pillows, and I drew a sketch of Athena, our insignia, which we framed and hung on the wall. With simple curtains for the windows, our lair was complete—almost.

All we needed was a phonograph and records. Mary Ann made a list of record requests, called a friend, and the phonograph and records arrived with surprising promptness. Now we had music—lots of it in fact—until the novelty wore off and the records got scratchy.

In late April or early May, I was assigned to the prosthetics department of the clinic, to work for Lt. R. Fishburn. Good-bye to the air and water hoses. Now I was mixing gooey stuff for impressions and keeping records of supplies, especially the gold, which had to be carefully accounted for. Not only was the new job more challenging, it was less tiring because I had opportunities to sit fairly often. Working in a room with just the dentist and the patient, I was less visible in my "blue rag." By then the weather was too warm to wear my trench coat, so I decided to wear my uniform to and from work and leave the rag at the clinic, making the necessary changes in our cloakroom. Nobody complained.

The 104th Division included units that used pack mules for carrying artillery pieces in mountainous terrain. The vocal cords of the mules had been cut so they wouldn't give away positions or movements to the enemy. In addition to carrying artillery, they pulled wagons of supplies. Eleanor Sneed was dating one of the mule packers, and one Sunday morning he arrived with two buddies, two mules, and a large wagon. They took us for a ride, which was bumpy but fun, then returned the mules and the wagon and came back in a jeep. We went out toward the mountains to a place with a bird's-eye view of the camp. It was strange to see the tiny speck that was our little WAC world in such a panoramic setting.

Not long afterward I received a small, soggy package in the mail. In it was a bouquet of lilies of the valley, wrapped in a wet cloth and waxed paper. With it was a damp but legible note from my mother saying that the flowers reminded her of little hands that brought them as offerings to her each spring. I felt homesick and nostalgic.

The startling news of the D day landings in Normandy on June 6 excited us tremendously. Although we were concerned about loved ones whom we feared might be involved, the general attitude was one of relief that at last things were moving. Those first few days we followed events on the radio in the day room and in whatever newspapers were available. LRs were abundant regarding the whereabouts of the 89th and 104th, which had shipped out earlier. The whole camp was stirring. Many of the hospital units moved out and more were preparing to do so.

The invasion renewed my interest in an overseas assignment. I decided to brave Lieutenant Herron, who was in charge of such matters, and make a request. Lieutenant Kathryn Herron, an attractive blonde who was confident and aware of her position, was reputably a formidable type. I must have caught her in the right mood. She listened carefully and seemed fairly receptive. She wanted to know where I was from. I told her that I was from upstate New York but had spent a lot of time in Pennsylvania because my parents were from there. She said she was from Pennsylvania and wanted to know where I'd lived. It turned out that her best friend was related to me—distantly, but I refrained from going into that. She was quite affable by then and told me she'd see what she could do. I left, confident that I hadn't muffed the interview but dubious as to whether it would reap any results.

After my talk with Lieutenant Herron, I was busy arranging for the three-day pass for which I was eligible. I contacted Anne, who was now in Biggs Field, Texas, to see if she could get one at the same time and meet me in Albuquerque. Her answer came by telegram on June 8:

HAVE PASS ARRIVE IN ALBUQUERQUE 625 AM
SUNDAY
WIRE AS TO WHEN YOU ARRIVE AND WHERE TO
MEET
ANNE

Evelyn Searls decided to go with me, and we took the *Atcheson, Topeka & Santa Fe* down to New Mexico. We met Anne at the El Fidel Hotel, where we had booked rooms. It was good to see Anne in uniform and hear about her army experiences in basic, which she'd taken at Fort Oglethorpe, and her assignment in the AirWAC at Biggs Field.

We took a short excursion to the Isleta Indian Reservation. The desert setting and the adobe architecture excited my romantic imagination, which carried me to Spain, the Sahara, and the Middle East. Anne took a picture of Evelyn and me sitting by an old wall. We took other pictures, too, of each other and of us with some little Indian boys who were following us around.

I'd never seen adobe structures before, so it was interesting to find out how durable and efficient they were. Not only was the church made of adobe, but much of it had been built at the time of the Pilgrims' arrival. The one-story houses with their flat roofs and rough-hewn vega poles, and the round outdoor bread ovens, blended with the buff-colored sand and seemed to grow from it. It was like a day out of time in a strange, quiet world.

At night we went to the Albuquerque USO club, which was large enough to offer all the amenities but small enough to be personal and friendly. We danced and played pool with the GIs.

One afternoon we were window-shopping and had stopped to look at the displays. Two women who were standing nearby apparently had been looking us over, and I heard one say, "I wonder which one is the madam?" So much for doing one's bit for the cause.

My long-awaited call came one morning after I'd returned from Albuquerque. I was working at the clinic and was told to report to Lieutenant Herron immediately. I hardly had time to be excited before I was in her office. She told me I was being sent to a signal corps school in preparation for a classified overseas assignment—every Wac's dream. My mind raced with the prospect of mystery and adventure—would there be palm trees and golden sands, or the quaint, ancient buildings of Europe, with maybe a bombing thrown in that I would safely survive? From somewhere in the distance, Lieutenant Herron's voice continued, ordering me to report at once to the hospital for a physical and shots.

There followed hectic hours during which I picked up my pay, laundry, and transportation vouchers, and went to the supply room where Gracie Hines issued me a full overseas kit. It included a duffel bag, winter clothing, and four-buckle overshoes. I had to have all of the clothing marked and laid out for an inspection the next morning, then have it packed so I could leave on the noon train. I wasn't even sure where I was going. The orders indicated Vint Hill Farms, Virginia, but nobody had ever heard of it. A portion of my orders, which were secret, was blocked out. I looked at my transportation ticket, which took me to Calverton, Virginia, via Washington, D.C., but none of us could find Calverton on the map.

Lieutenant Mazzei had given me a delay en route, so I was bound for Rochester, via Chicago, on the faithful Rocket. The weather was hot; my arms were red, sore, and swollen from the shots; and there were no seats available on the train. Soldiers spilled over the seats and into the aisles. I found a space between the cars that I shared with a GI as ingenious as I. We rode, sitting on our suitcases, the soot drifting down and the couplings jolting every now and then as the prairie whirred by. At Omaha we beat the mob and found seats.

Pleased for the chance to show off my beautiful new sun-tan uniforms during my brief delay en route, I took Mom to dinner at O'Leary's Chop House in East Rochester, and I visited neighbors and other friends as far away as Friendship.

The night I left, Mom cooked a special meal, which included my favorite pork loin chops, and we ate it on the front porch because of the hot weather. Then it was time for me to go. Marie, who was probably tired from working the night shift at Kodak, didn't want to take me to the train station in the city. Daddy, disgusted with her, said he'd take me, even though he too had been working a night shift and managing the farm as well. Mom kissed me and said, "Good-bye, darlin'." For a moment a strange premonition swept over me—a feeling that something would happen and I'd never see her again. Then Daddy took me to the train station and kissed me good-bye, the only time I ever remember his kissing me. Because he wasn't known to be demonstrative, it occurred to me that he thought I might be killed overseas. I didn't think that likely, but I was moved.

It was a relief to be on the train and moving again, with my good-byes behind me. I went on to Washington, where I spent the rest of the night before taking the train for Virginia the next morning.

The crowded train made frequent stops as it crawled southward through the lush countryside. I hadn't any idea how long the trip was going to take because none of the GIs around me had heard of Calverton. When the conductor came through calling, "Next stop, Calverton," I couldn't picture any sizable place coming up in all that flat farming country. Well, there wasn't any sizable place—just one tiny station house, hardly larger than an outhouse.

Expecting to be the only one getting off, I was surprised to see two Wac privates, whom I hadn't noticed, leaving the train. One turned to me and said, "Are you getting off here, corporal?" Sue Cross was attractive, about my height, with sandy hair, and seemed alert, intelligent, and self-assured. Her companion, Violet "Vi" Flower, was shorter and slightly plump with a round, cheerful face, blue eyes, and a slight British accent. Later, I was to call her Posy. The three of us were to be members of a small group that was never separated, night or day, until after the war.

We didn't know what to do. The place was deserted except for the stationmaster, who was exactly the stereotype one would expect, with his green scoop eyeshade and glasses that had slipped down his nose. He'd been expecting us and told us that someone would come in from the camp and pick us up. Meanwhile, we could go across the road to the store and get some pop to cool off.

We crossed the narrow dirt road to a tiny general store that stood under a tall tree. An old collie was dozing in the shade, and it was so quiet we could hear the flies buzzing. We drank orange pop and got acquainted while we waited.

Then we heard a truck approaching along the road beyond the station, and a three-quarter-ton army pickup came into view, leaving a small cloud of dust in its wake. It wasn't the transportation expected for three people, but it was better than the usual two-and-a-half-ton truck. The driver loaded our things, and we climbed in and sat down on the parallel benches along the sides of the truck bed. The canopy was on but we could see out the back as we wound our way through semiwooded country. The road became narrower, with grass growing between the tracks, and we joked that supplies probably had to be parachuted in. Then we saw the radio towers, lots of them, tall and relatively close together. In a short time we were at the gate, where identifications were definitely scrutinized. We were at Vint Hill.

In uniform at last. Fort Devens, 1943.

July 1943. Day two, Fort Devens, Massachusetts. I'm the fourth in the second row.

"Here we stand like birds in the wilderness. . . ." Beside the mess hall, Fort Devens.

Second Officer Gerlach, our genial company commander at Fort Devens.

"Edible? Who'd wanna eat dat stuff?"

Barracks #1642, my special home at Camp Carson, Colorado. August 1943.

Mt. Cheyenne, September 1943. Near the Will Rogers shrine.

Eager and idealistic, I pose for a portrait to send home. October 1943.

Evelyn Searls, Eleanor Sneed, and Loretta Townsend, with whom I shared many good times at Camp Carson.

Incomparable Mary Ann. Her unpredictable comments kept us in stitches.

Our Strictly GI first sergeant Harlee with company commander Lieutenant Mazzei.

A pause in preparation for Saturday inspection.

All smiles, the Camp Carson gang in our Sunday best with me front and center.

"Parade rest" drill time, after a day's work.

Thanksgiving Day Parade, Colorado Springs, 1943.

Some of my friends ready to brave the crowded P.X.

On furlough, January 1944.

Women's stripes were full-sized,
unlike those of today.

My sister Ann on furlough from Biggs Field, Texas. October 1944.

Displaying my new stripes, February 1944.

Three

Vint Hill Farms was unlike anything I had imagined. Was it a farm, or wasn't it? It was set among trees and cultivated fields like any other farm in the region. There was the usual farm complex—a large, two-story house and an impressive barn with associated buildings—but there were more buildings than would normally be found on a farm, some camouflaged and tucked away among the trees of an orchard. Military personnel, singly or in pairs, moved here and there. It was a post, but it was designed to attract as little attention as possible when viewed from the air. I learned later that the farmhouse served as headquarters, the barn was the operations-communications center, and the other buildings included a PX, a theater, and a dispensary. One of the huts in the orchard was our classroom, and I assumed that the others were used for similar purposes.

We arrived at the WAC orderly room, which along with the day room and mess hall, stood on one side of a graveled area. On the other side were one-story barracks behind which was a field of neatly cultivated beans that came right to the barrack's back doors. We were housed in one of the barracks along with girls from the regular detachment. Unlike Camp Carson where we had our own cots, the Vint Hill Wacs had double bunks, undoubtedly to conserve space. The detachment had some 160 people, and for security reasons the fewer the buildings the better.

When we arrived at our barracks, we were met with a much-appreciated welcome. Our bunks were already made up, with a penny for good luck under each pillow. Some girls from the regular detachment, thinking we were replacing them for overseas service, felt they could afford to be magnanimous. When they learned the bitter truth, they were no longer friendly.

After everyone in our special group arrived, we were summoned to the day room and given instructions. There were nineteen of us from most of the ten service commands into which the country had been divided. We would be the only Wacs ever to take the course.

The following two days were spent in processing—physicals at the dispensary, then on to military intelligence to sign forms, one of which dealt with the background of our parents. We were told that by the time we left, the government would know all about them. We also learned that four agencies were involved in our clearance: the FBI, military intelligence (G-2), post finance, and a private detective agency. We were warned never to divulge to anyone, GI or civilian, the name of the post or anything related to it. Later, Mary "Gremmy" Summerhalter told me the following:

> Vint Hill Farms was so top secret that once we left the station we never mentioned its name. One night while waiting for the bus to return us to Warrenton from Washington, D.C., Margie and I stood in line with a couple of army personnel. Conversation centered

around where we were stationed, with remarks like, "it's south of here . . . it's in Virginia . . . it's however many miles . . . [I don't remember how many miles]. Finally someone said, "Hell, let's admit it . . . we're all from Vint Hill Farms."

After the briefing, we went to be photographed for the brown ID buttons that were required to get on and off the post.

Classes began the following Monday on the principle of self-instruction via a training manual, with each person working at her own speed. We were graded, and anything lower than eighty-five had to be rewritten. The classes lasted for eight hours, except for lunch hour and time off for retreat, and were given six days a week.

We began with cryptography, which involved learning to encipher and decipher messages in code and cipher. Mastering a number of systems was only the beginning; we then had to learn to analyze them, because we were being trained as cryptanalysts. A cryptanalyst had the military occupational specialty (MOS) number 808, which was defined in a current army manual as follows:

Decodes and deciphers enemy messages and cryptograms without the aid of the device or key used in preparing them.

Using deductive reasoning and employing knowledge of the various cryptographic codes, analyzes messages and determines key to code.

May supervise others in cryptanalysis. Must have cryptographic clearance.

Must have training in cryptanalysis and be familiar with all types of cryptographic systems and their variations in military communications. Must possess initiative, patience, and marked deductive ability.

Should have some mathematical training and be familiar with at least one foreign language.

We practiced on messages used by the Union army at Gettysburg, because a similar encoding procedure was used by the Japanese in one of their shipping codes. We worked with only one machine, the M-209, a medium-level cryptographic system.

In addition, we had a daily class in Hepburn Kana, the system devised for converting the Japanese characters into syllables—a necessity for transmitting the language in Morse code. We learned a lot of Japanese military vocabulary and the grammatical structures we'd be likely to encounter in their messages. We "assumed" (a word used frequently by cryptanalysts, and jokingly among ourselves) that we'd be going to the Pacific, but we dared tell no one. Those skeptics among us, knowing the way the army could operate, wouldn't have been surprised if we were headed for Europe.

I didn't mention that each one of us was dismissed from class for KP, corporals as well as privates. Nowhere in the army did I ever encounter such a disorganized, disgraceful mess. My colleagues emphatically agreed. The WAC officer in charge was either appallingly incompetent or powerless to do anything about it. Instead of having trays, plates and other dishes were used, which kept the KPs slaving from five o'clock in the morning until nine or later at night. If the work was finished before preparations for the next meal were begun, there would be a ten- to fifteen-minute break.

Fortunately, I was on it only once. The grease trap detail involved using a No. 10 can to skim the foul, rancid-smelling grease from the plumbing trap and pouring it into a container. Cleaning the grease trap climaxed a duty from which it took two days to recover.

Because of our grueling schedule, we stayed close to camp during the week, going to the PX or relaxing in the barracks. Occasionally, I'd go into the USO at "Warren Green" in nearby Warrenton, not far from Manassas, where the battle of Bull Run was fought during the Civil War. Warrenton was also in the heart of the "horse country," and I took in a horse show one day.

Because we were close to Washington, Sue, Vi, and I seized the opportunity to sign up for passes to go there. We arrived at noon and got a pleasant room in a tourist home recommended by one of the Vint Hill Farms (VHF) girls. That afternoon we went to the Army Medical Museum (Sue and Vi had been medical technicians) and the Smithsonian, after which we had dinner at a Mayflower cafe.

I went into Washington only once after that. I hadn't seen much the first time, so I decided to see some of the historic sights and meet Arianna Wight, with whom I had shared a KP stint at Camp Carson. I was homesick for the gang there.

I attended a starlight concert in Meridian Hill Park and took a boat trip on the Potomac, passing Mount Vernon, which was lighted despite the war. Gliding along the river was cool and relaxing.

On another occasion I went with the group to Arlington Hall, Virginia, for a special ceremony. One of us, Pfc. Mary Jane Ford, was being awarded the Soldier's Medal for risking her life to save a drowning GI while at Camp McCoy, Wisconsin. Jane had been on the edge of a small lake near the camp when she noticed a young man who was in apparent trouble. She jumped in and swam to where he was thrashing in the water, but he sank, pulling her down with him. Despite his size—six feet two inches and about 180 pounds—

she managed to get him back to shore, where she applied artificial respiration and sent someone for help. They were unable to save him.

For Jane, receiving the medal was an ordeal. An introverted type, she had difficulty dealing with the media, numerous dignitaries, and the grieving parents of the young man. For the rest of us it was exciting. We formed the honor guard of the parade and had a firsthand view of the ceremony in which the general pinned the medal on her chest. We were proud because she was one of only ten Wacs ever to receive the medal, and she was one of *us*. I think that marked the real beginning of our feeling as a special "family."

Most of us were very close. We argued and quarreled like sisters, laughed, and closed ranks against outsiders in defense of any member. That's the way it was then, and that's the way it was the day we got together again for the first time thirty-seven years later. (I've included my impression of each member of the "family" in an appendix.)

Shortly before leaving Vint Hill, I began to skip retreat. Having to march across a rough field to music emanating from a distant loudspeaker, with a company of Wacs whom I didn't know, had become a chore. I didn't anticipate a problem by missing retreat. Wednesday afternoons when it was held, everyone was excused a little early to get back to the area, form the platoons, and march onto the field. There wasn't time for roll call. Apparently others before me had made the same decision. Suspicious NCOs, noticing the thinning ranks, had begun quick searches of the barracks, so I had to be careful. They had already nabbed a number of us from the showers and clothes closets. But I had a better idea. By now the beans in the field behind the barracks were luxuriant, so I slipped out and lay down between the rows until the detachment marched away. My scheme was foolproof.

One night after the girls had vacated the barracks, I went out and sat on the back steps. A large yellow moon dominated the sky behind the row of trees that bordered the bean field. The air was warm and humid and heavy with the scent of green growing things. Somewhere in the lush meadows beyond the trees, frogs piped a steady, melancholy chorus. The serenity was complete. I felt an inexpressible sadness, a longing for an intangible something I couldn't define, something of the long ago and far away that lingered on the fragile edge of memory.

Finally, the last classes were over. We said our good-byes to Sergeant Nelson, our "keeper," and to Tokashi Kajihara, the nisei who taught us Japanese. The next morning, September 16, we boarded trucks and left Vint Hill behind us. It was 8:30 A.M. on a Saturday. We had to wait until 4:30 P.M. before we could get on the train for Chattanooga. From there we'd be going to Fort Oglethorpe for overseas training.

The train huffed and puffed its way southwestward. Despite the heat and the drifting soot, our spirits were high and we were eager to get on with it. Night came, then dawn, and in our impatience we wondered if the war would be over before we got there. Then, at last—Chattanooga. It was 9:30 A.M. on Sunday.

Four

Fort Oglethorpe dates back to the early years of the twentieth century when the 7th Cavalry was first stationed there. During World War I, the fort was a training center; it had a base hospital for treating casualties, and a German war prisoner barracks that remained there several years after the war ended. Now, a Class I installation, Fort Oglethorpe was an Armed Forces Induction Center and the 3d WAC Training Center. Here too, was the Officer Candidate School (OCS) for the WAC and an area set aside for the extended field service (EFS) program.

A truck picked us up at Chattanooga and took us directly to the EFS area, which we reached around noon. We grabbed a bite to eat, then were marched off to lectures even though it was Sunday. It was 6:00 P.M. before we had supper and took a shower. We were to discover that this would be the normal pace for the next two weeks.

The following day each of us was issued the one pair of coveralls that would be our uniform for the entire training period. I got mine down to size with safety pins. We never dared wash them because they'd never dry enough to put on the next morning. Although the weather wasn't particularly hot, it was muggy and sticky. After exercising and tramping around in the dirt, we didn't even want to touch them, let alone put them on.

Training consisted of lectures, movies, rugged physical training (PT) exercises, climbing a cargo net, a quick exposure to gas in a gas chamber, and a long hike with a full pack. (Wacs weren't allowed to have firearms, so instruction in their use was not included.) The training lasted eight hours a day, seven days a week, and involved a battalion of Wacs, roughly 250 people. I expected to be in poor physical shape after ten weeks of sitting in the classroom at Vint Hill without much exercise. Although we'd had PT there, I had done it in the rear ranks of the platoon where my half-hearted efforts wouldn't be noticed by the sergeant. Even so, I did exceptionally well. I didn't get sore or tired and I discovered I was enjoying the training.

I looked forward to climbing the cargo net. My enthusiasm may have been due to newsreels that showed soldiers climbing cargo nets. More likely, it was the girls talking about how difficult it was. I was eager to meet the challenge. The appointed day came. Wearing our steel helmets and backpacks, we were marched to the area where the net of heavy ropes hung over each side of a wall fifteen to twenty feet high. I was disappointed—it didn't look high enough.

We were lined up in three or four columns; when the sergeant blew her whistle, the first girl in each column ran, grasped the net, and started climbing. When they'd climbed high enough so they wouldn't kick the next one in the face, the sergeant would send off another group. Of course there were the usual klutzes who got stuck so that people bunched up and the sergeant yelled to get on with it. I took careful aim to avoid those when my turn came, and I went over easily.

While waiting on the other side of the wall for the rest to get over, I noticed a familiar figure resting in the shade of the net. It was Genks (Helen Genkins), one of our group, a quietly amiable girl from Iowa. In her soft midwestern drawl she told me she hadn't gone over. Everybody had been so busy watching the nets that she'd slipped around the side and found shade for a little snooze.

Another exercise was going through the gas chamber so we would know what to do in case of a gas attack. The gas chamber was a building with a door on each end. With a gas mask on, we went up the steps to the door, where an NCO admitted us, one by one, into the chamber. We then walked to the center of the room, roughly the size of a living room, where we were instructed to remove the mask, quickly take a whiff of the gas, and replace the mask. It wasn't necessary to add "quickly." This accomplished, we walked out the door on the other side.

I enjoyed the field hike most of all. We wore steel helmets rather than the usual helmet liners and carried a full load, including rations, in our backpacks, or musette bags, as they were called. The musette bag was held in place by straps that cut into our shoulders, so we stuffed Kotex under them to prevent blisters.

We set off, marching along a dirt road on our way out of the post. We'd been told to be ready at any moment for air raid alerts, at which time we were to scatter for cover and throw ourselves flat on the ground. Talking and singing were prohibited, so all we could hear was the steady tramping of feet. On each side of us were occasional bushes or shrubs, some of which grew close to ditches along the edge of the road. Farther back were trees that thickened into a wood.

Suddenly, the whistle blew. I'd been eyeing my side of the road and lost no time diving under a bush. There weren't enough bushes for everyone, so some collided while heading for the same cover. Sensible ones threw themselves flat into the ditches, but others were running around like scattered chickens bemoaning the fact that there was no place to "hide." The sergeants were disgusted and told us that the whole stupid lot of us were going to get ourselves killed.

We came into Chickamauga National Military Park, which commemorated the battle fought in 1863, eighty-one years before almost to the day. We passed cannon and a number of statues and monuments honoring the Confederate states and their units who fought there. When we stopped to eat, I took a close look at the nearest monument.

I was momentarily transported in space and time to Freewill Number 8, the little district school where I read everything I could find about the Civil War. Pubescently romantic, I had longed to live in those times or visit the historic places, never dreaming I'd be in one of them, about to go into the unknown of the biggest war of all.

When we got back to the barracks late that afternoon, it felt good to get rid of the packs and straps. We'd hiked between ten and fourteen miles, the estimates varied depending largely on the relative fatigue of the estimators.

The last night before leaving Oglethorpe was hectic; we had to pack everything we'd been issued into one barracks bag and one duffel bag. Compulsively, I had my things in sized piles and arranged in some order so I could get at what I would most likely need. There wasn't much room left after my buckle overshoes, bathrobe, overcoat, and other heavy items were packed. There were both summer and winter blouses and skirts, shirts, and underclothes besides the few things we needed and could put in the musette bag for the train journey. Most were stuffable, but what was I to do with my Hobby hat to keep it from being crushed? Nearly everyone preferred the overseas cap, but I clung tenaciously and loyally to what I considered the last remaining item of the dress uniform that was uniquely WAC. At Vint Hill I wore it and my shirts with the 7th Service Command patches everywhere I went. I wound up stuffing the hat with underwear and cradling it among larger items in the duffel bag.

The next morning we fell out in full gear and marched to the railhead a couple of miles away at the edge of the post. Our packs were heavy with all we'd managed to cram into them. The steel helmets we were required to wear added to our load, but we hardly noticed in our excitement to be on our way.

Just as we reached the crest of the hill above the railhead, we could see the waiting train about a half mile below. Beside it was a little band. Suddenly the band struck up an old British army tune, "Colonel Bogey," made famous later in the movie *The Bridge on the River Kwai*. Spontaneously, we sang the WAC words:

> *Duty is calling you and me*
> *We have a date with destiny*
> *Ready, our hearts are ready*
> *Our pulses steady,*
> *The world to set free!*
> *Win it! We're in it heart and soul*
> *Victory will be our only goal*
> *We love our country's honor*
> *And we'll defend it against every foe!*

Nothing could have thrilled us more deeply than the stirring music and words of that song. For me, those moments on the crest of a hill in Georgia were a high point in my army experience.

We boarded the train alphabetically, car by car, not knowing our destination. LRs, mainly the product of wishful thinking, intimated that we were going to the European theater of operations (ETO). Smugly, we 808s (cryptanalysts) knew it should be the other direction because of our training in Japanese, but knowing the capricious ways of the army, we couldn't be sure. Why the overcoats, fur-lined field jackets, and four-buckle overshoes? Why, too, were we heading north? Alaska? Although it wouldn't have been too bad if we wound up in the ETO, we regarded Alaska as a catastrophe. It had to be the Pacific. I was all set for palm trees and tropic isles, a dream ever since I'd read Frederick O'Brien's *White Shadows in the South Seas.*

The train chugged along for a couple of hours and then veered into the lowering sun. Relief—we were westward bound.

The cars were a Pullman type with one upper bunk and a lower one that had to be shared. I was assigned to the latter, along with an older, somewhat plump Wac named Zoe Brown, who took up more than half the bed. She wasn't even an interesting conversationalist.

Because of the alphabetizing, our group was strung out all the way to the last car. One of my best friends, Harriott Bell, was with me in the first one. Harriott was adventurous and innovative, had a good sense of humor, and was interested in English literature and poetry.

Prohibited from leaving the assigned cars, we missed our friends and had to devise ways to get back to the other coaches. Harriott came up with a clever idea—we would offer our services to the friendly but naive special services officer, Lieutenant Chave. It was Lieutenant Chave's duty to keep up our morale during the trip by doling out goodies such as gum, candy bars, packets of crackers, and magazines each day, after which she disappeared until the next morning. Bell and I (the army used surnames; there were too many Helens, Marys, et cetera, so the names stuck, especially if they were short) eagerly offered to distribute the items for her. "How nice, it's so good of you to do this," she said. Our haloes glistened. She'd leave us to our task, which took up the entire morning, ending exactly at lunchtime.

Every once in a while, the train stopped and we had to wait until it was shunted to another track. If time permitted, we had to fall out and do PT. Often there'd be other troop trains alongside us crammed with GIs, who hung out of the windows, chatting, joking, and showing off. There were no nasty or abusive remarks, just a good feeling of friendliness and camaraderie.

After a couple of days, the special service goodies were depleted and we had to devise a new means to get back through the cars. We'd had to crawl around people near the end of the train, waiting in line for sick call, so I decided a migraine or two might be in order. After receiving the army's cure-all pills, APCs, we could take our time getting back to our coach. However, as the trip wore on, the sick-call line got longer and the medics fussier, making it risky to use illness as an excuse to visit our friends. We settled on going to the latrine car, where we could pass the time viewing the countryside from a large observation window and chat with whomever came in.

As we passed through the Rockies, the mountains seemed more spectacular than ever, and I gave way to moments of nostalgia. Not far away was Camp Carson, where my old friends would be working in their offices or hovering over dental chairs. I visualized drills boring down into scores of GI teeth. The nostalgia rapidly vanished.

We left the high Rockies behind us, passing through the tablelands at Grand Junction and on across the salt flats of Utah into Nevada. By then it was night, clear and crisply cool. On the horizon to the north was a low black range of mountains, surprisingly visible although there was no moon. I heard the plaintive howl of a coyote somewhere in the distance.

Camp Stoneman, California
October 5–10, 1944

The two West Coast points of embarkation (POEs) for army personnel being shipped to the Pacific theater were Seattle and Camp Stoneman, near Pittsburg, California. When we left Salt Lake City and headed westward into Nevada, rather than northwest toward Idaho where the main lines connect for Seattle, we knew we were California bound.

Camp Stoneman was alive with activity—troops marching in all directions; trucks, jeeps, and assorted army vehicles on the move; and men of all ranks hurrying determinedly toward designated places. This was war, and Camp Stoneman was a point of embarkation. Our EFS battalion was stuffed into barracks containing bunks and a latrine with inadequate facilities.

I had washing to do so I entered the latrine. All of the sinks were occupied, but I noticed a strange elongated one where there was still available space. Then I discovered it had no faucets. How odd. And no plugs, either. Two girls were engaged in pouring water from No. 10 cans over their clothes, so I found a can and filled it with water from a shower. Hurrying back to the bizarre "sink" where my filthy herringbone twills (HBTs) awaited me, I dicovered that my No. 10 can had a hole near the bottom from which water was spraying—on a passing Wac wearing a newly pressed skirt. She restrained from strangling me. Such was my introduction to a urinal.

Although we were going to be at Camp Stoneman for only a few days, the extensive training we had to undergo required several articles of clothing that we had crammed into our duffel bags at Fort Oglethorpe. Had we been told in advance what we would need at Camp Stoneman, we would have packed accordingly. Therefore, we had to take everything out of the bags to get at the required items. A few days later, we had to repack, a job that took the entire evening before our departure.

The training was similar to that at Fort Oglethorpe—lectures; PT; blue, green, and red "alerts"; and how to dig a slit trench, an outdoor latrine. Instruction in the latter was given by a black male sergeant, which surprised us, because the races were separated in the World War II army.

In addition to the training, we had physicals, more shots, and a "bug" inspection, which was humiliating. We were each taken into a small room to disrobe. Then we were examined with a flashlight, first our undies and then us, in regions where little creatures were most likely to be found.

Finally we had to pack everything again, with one added ghoulish item, a "mattress" bag, for a corpse should we have the misfortune to become one.

Before leaving, on the morning of October 10, we went to services in our respective denominational chapels. As I sang the old familiar hymn "Jesus, Savior, Pilot Me," thoughts of home, mixed with the awareness of possible dangers ahead, were overshadowed by my excitement at going overseas.

After all the warnings about secrecy, we marched through the town of Pittsburg in broad daylight, passing a school where children were having noon recess. Some waved to us, but most were preoccupied with their play. As we approached the docks to board the ferry for San Francisco, we sang our words to "California Here We Come":

> *Gangplank, gangplank, here we come*
> *Away from where we started from*
> *We're going, we're going, we're going overseas*
> *Get ready, get ready, look out you Nipponese!*
> *Oh gangplank, gangplank we are here*
> *We won't be back for another year*
> *But when we do we want that cheer—*
> *California, here we co-o-me!*

We debarked at the Embarcadero where the Red Cross supplied us with coffee and doughnuts and a little ditty bag of useful items.

Our ship, the *Lurline,* loomed huge before us. I had never seen such a gigantic one. In fact, the only boat I'd ever encountered was the ferry that I once took across Lake Ontario.

As I went up the gangplank, I heard a band on the dock playing "Mairzy Doats" and "Is You Is or Is You Ain't My Baby?" The selections were hardly appropriate for such a momentous occasion. Enlisted personnel directed us below to our "staterooms" on D deck, way down in the hold.

I deposited my gear in the tiny cabin that I was to share with eight others and went up to the promenade deck to look around. The *Lurline,* I learned, exceeded two football fields in length, although it didn't seem that big once I was aboard. Along with its sister ship, the *Matsonia,* and two smaller ships the *Mariposa* and the *Monterey,* it was one of the luxury liners of the Matson Line. Immediately following the Pearl Harbor attack, they had been converted to troop carriers and carried Wacs, nurses, battle casualties, and Red Cross workers as well as various troops and military personnel.

The ship now bore little resemblance to its former self. Nowhere was this more evident than in the Grand Ballroom, which was crammed with rows of bunks that seemed to rise to the ceiling. Gone were the chandeliers, overstuffed furniture, and other trappings that had contributed to the elegant surroundings and comfort of the traveler.

It took hours to load the troops and get them settled in. The process was still going on when I crawled into my top bunk that night. The ceiling was so close that I had to slide in sideways, and after I had positioned myself with my life preserver as bedfellow, I could scarcely lift my head. There was a ventilator directly above my face, but it was no longer operable, so I knew that when we reached the tropics, I would be very uncomfortable.

We still hadn't started before I fell asleep. Then, early in the morning, the motion of the ship awakened me. At last we were under way.

Five

"Now hear this . . ." The public address (PA) system was one thing on the ship that worked. The navy began all announcements in this way, and that first morning they proceeded to give directions for going to breakfast. I took my mess kit and went down to the dining area below us, on E deck. The room was large. The chow line ran along one side, and long tables filled the rest of the room except for a roped-off area of small tables that were reserved for officers.

Boiled potato was slapped into my mess kit. I went to a table, sat down, and took a bite of it, at which point I was hit with a wave of nausea. Remembering that the best solution for the problem was fresh air, I rushed up to the promenade deck with record speed and headed for the rail. The air momentarily revived me so that I swallowed the potato, but I wasn't inclined to eat anything until late that afternoon when someone gave me cheese and crackers. From then on I was fine, but I stayed up on deck for the rest of the day.

We spent most of our time on the promenade deck, where we met our friends and had a little more space than in our staterooms. I say "a little more space" because everyone else had the same idea.

Our rooms, which were about fifteen feet square and intended for one or two people, had nine, along with bags and gear. Three-tiered bunks stood against three sides of the room, and the door to the one toilet opened off the fourth. Duffel and barracks bags were stacked, and helmets and musette bags hung from the posts of the bunks. There was an open space about four feet square.

Those first nights, when I was still sleeping in my bunk, I could feel the ship slowly leaning, creaking as it did so, until it seemed that it was going to turn completely over. Then it would slowly start back in the opposite direction. I gradually became accustomed to the motion, like a giant comforting cradle, and would drift back to sleep.

Regulations aboard ship were few but of vital importance, and for the most part we obeyed them without question. We had to be extremely careful not to let anything fall overboard, because a trail of debris could be followed by Japanese submarines, always a potential danger. Therefore, books, papers, playing cards, and games weren't permitted on the open decks, and people who smoked were forbidden to throw their butts overboard. Smoking on the decks after dusk wasn't permitted because all sources of light had to be extinguished.

We had to have our life preservers (Mae Wests) with us at all times and were told never to sit on them or use them as pillows; this would pack down the kapok and destroy its buoyancy. Most of us conveniently "forgot" that rule; pillows weren't allowed on deck, and the temptation to use the preservers was too hard to resist. As we approached the equator the heat of the cabins became unbearable, and most of us slept on the decks wherever we could find a place and not be stepped on.

Fresh water was at a premium. With some 5,000 people aboard, we were lucky to have an allowance of one helmetful a day. The helmet fit nicely in the toilet seat, where it served as a sink. First we'd take a sponge bath and then use the water to wash our clothes. Clothes meant shirts and undies, not our one pair of HBT slacks. We had to sleep in those when up on deck. There was adequate saltwater for rinsing clothes and taking showers, but the results of the latter were unsatisfactory. Ordinary soap was impossible, and saltwater soap wasn't much better, so shaving cream was used until the PX supply was exhausted after a few days. Whenever we used the showers, we shed flakes of salt after we dried off.

Besides having to keep out of restricted areas, one of which was the sundeck, reserved for officers, the only other rule was a ten-minute time limit on eating. We ate only twice a day because of the logistics of feeding so many people, and we felt deprived of savoring our food such as it was. The food became increasingly worse as the days went by. Once I was sitting at a table right next to the officer's roped-off dining area. Across the rope were officers eating at a small table, so close I could almost reach out and help myself to fried chicken and a glass of cold tomato juice. In my mess kit was a large blob of unwatered pea soup that one of the cooks splatted in my direction as I passed down the chow line. The usual marine was patrolling our aisles and bellowing, "Eat, don't talk!" Suddenly I was furious over the injustice of it all. Here we were supposed to be saving democracy, and privilege was extended in an area that had nothing to do with army discipline.

On another occasion we were served pigs' knuckles with the bristles sticking out of the skins. For Harriot Bell it was the last straw. She wrote her mother a letter filled with vitriolic complaints that caught the censor's eye. She was called in, lectured, and assigned to a detail of scrubbing one of the companionway walls. When we heard of this latest injustice, some of us got together to help. We vented our spleen in a bitch session as we scrubbed, and in no time the job was done.

Once we were served something that apparently wasn't fresh, and scores were struck with the GIs (diarrhea). All of the ship's hospital beds were full. Bell and I, who were less afflicted, stood in line for our doses of paregoric and bismuth, the military's panacea for this particular disorder. We made a quick recovery.

Entertainment was adequate to keep everybody from being bored during the long days of a long journey, especially under such crowded conditions. There was a troupe from the GI musical *Yanksapoppin* that performed selections from their show, and special services put together programs and skits on deck and in one of the foyers. The skits were under the direction of a Lieutenant Budd, who led us in singing as well. He seemed especially fond of "I Wanna Go Back to Where I Come From," which, like "Someone's in the Kitchen with Dinah," always succeeded in setting my teeth on edge.

Movies were shown in the dining room. *The Sullivans* was a true story about five brothers who enlisted in the navy together and went down on the same ship. No one seemed to mind the morbid plot.

In a small room off the deck was a piano where one GI played classical music exceptionally well. His extensive repertoire included English folk songs, of which he was fond. Some of us would rush to grab one of the few straight-back chairs in the room so we could listen in style. Except for our ten-minute meals, this was the only chance we had to sit on a chair. It was a luxury after the hard decks. (I rarely got one of the scarce chairs, and if I did, I felt guilty and shared it.) Once, I summoned up my nerve and requested a selection of Brahms. The pianist practically spat with contempt. Apparently, Brahms was not "in" among the musical cognoscenti. I never forgot how humiliated I felt. After that, I could no longer enjoy his music completely.

Although books could be checked out of the ship's donated collection, reading was virtually impossible because of the constant distractions of people stepping over me as they passed by. Most of the time was spent moving around seeking our friends, chatting, and exchanging the latest LRs. Some sat in the foyers and companionways and wrote letters or played cards.

Sue, Marge, Bell, and I played bridge day after day, until visions of cards floated before my eyes as I fell asleep. The games often erupted into arguments, some of which got pretty voluble. Neither Sue nor Bell had doubts about their convictions. Marge and I usually listened, enjoying the action, and then Marge, cool and logical, would state her opinion, the matter would simmer down, and we'd go back to the game.

I spent a lot of time at the rail, watching the ocean. It was such a rich cobalt blue—the color of the bluing my mother used in the rinse water when she was doing laundry. The ocean extended on all sides of the ship to the horizon. I gazed at it day after day for nearly three weeks. October is a month of swells in the South Pacific. Gigantic rounded mountains of them kept coming on, seeming to completely engulf us. Then, with the gentlest motion, they passed under the ship and the next one approached. I was awed and mesmerized.

Between the periods of the gigantic swells there'd be occasional schools of flying fish rising in graceful arcs from the water and slipping back in again without leaving a trace.

From those momentary glimpses of life in that immensity of ocean, I was struck by the vastness of what lay below: whole mountain ranges created when the earth was born. The cosmic connections absorbed me.

At night, when I stood at the rail of the darkened ship and looked at the ocean, I was equally enchanted. Reflected light from the sky defined the edges of the waves or the contours of the swells so I could trace them as they approached. Great patches of phosphorus glowed and sparkled on the blackness of the water. I could understand how man, across the ages, had fallen under the spell of the sea.

Once we ran into a storm that cleared the decks of everyone except a few of us who didn't get sick and wanted to stay and watch its fury. Here was the dark side of the ocean that prompted the words to the stirring navy hymn "Eternal Father Strong to Save":

> *Eternal Father, strong to save*
> *Whose arm doth bind the restless wave*
> *Who bidst the mighty ocean deep*
> *Its own appointed limits keep*
> *Oh, hear us when we cry to Thee*
> *For those in peril on the sea.*

Services were held on deck each morning, and whenever we sang that hymn, I was reminded of that stormy afternoon.

The ship steamed across the Pacific in a zigzag pattern, changing direction every seven minutes. It was estimated that by the time a sub could set its sights and fire, the ship would have turned and the torpedoes would have run parallel to and away from the ship. We never saw any subs, but once we were ordered to our cabins, where we could hear the ship's guns firing. Someone told us that the crew was having gunnery practice.

October 25 was eventful for two reasons: it was my birthday, and we sighted land for the first time since San Francisco. Everyone ran to one side of the ship on hearing the news. There, far on the horizon, was the dark, mountainous island of New Caledonia rising slowly out of the sea. After a while it loomed large in front of us as we headed for the harbor at Noumea. Rounding the southern tip of the island, we passed a tiny gem of an isle on our port side. It was an idyllic scene, all brilliance and color—the stark white lighthouse, the turquoise-aquamarine water, and the little red roofs of houses emerging from the jungle green vegetation just beyond the rim of pale sand along the shore.

As we pulled into the harbor and dropped anchor, some GIs, muscular torsos golden from the tropic sun, drew alongside the ship in little white boats and waved to us. We spent the afternoon and night there, but then left. The war was awaiting us somewhere else, and we left without ever knowing why we had stopped.

We had known for some time that we were probably going to Australia. There were a lot of Wacs in Brisbane, where MacArthur's general headquarters (GHQ) for the whole South Pacific was located, so we assumed that would be our destination. A day or so before we expected to land we were paid in Australian currency. That clinched it. At the same time, *A Pocket Guide to New Guinea,* one of the armed service pocketbooks, was distributed to most of the men. One section issued a warning about leeches that drop from leaves in the jungle:

> They will probably get in through your skin no matter what you wear. If allowed to bloat up on your blood they will drop off. Get rid of them as soon as you can. But never tear them off, as a bad sore may result. A lighted cigarette, a cigarette lighter, a spit of tobacco juice, soapy water, gasoline, or a pinch of salt are used to make leeches let go. . . .

We shuddered, offering the men our condolences, relieved that we'd be debarking in Brisbane soon.

At last the announcement was made that we'd be arriving the next afternoon. Like waiting for Santa Claus, it seemed the morrow would never come. Then, around ten o'clock the next morning we were summoned and informed that because of the Leyte campaign that had recently begun, Brisbane harbor was so congested that we'd be unable to land in Australia. All personnel would continue on the ship to New Guinea.

The armed service pocket guide indicated that New Guinea was truly tropical. Despite the leech warning, I was glad to be going there. I was still dreaming of a tropical paradise, especially after seeing New Caledonia. Moreover, New Guinea was closer to the war.

As the ship turned northwest and entered the Coral Sea, the ocean suddenly changed from brilliant blue to gray, and increasing numbers of cumulus clouds floated languorously across the sky. It seemed to be hotter and more humid than ever, and everyone was restless and eager to get off the ship. There were few LRs regarding our specific destination in New Guinea and how long it would take to get there, probably because of our complete ignorance of the geography of the region. Consequently, our first sight of the island came as a surprise.

Milne Bay, Papua, New Guinea
ca. October 30, 1944

Milne Bay, located at the southernmost tip of the Australian territory of Papua, accommodated ships of all sizes en route to and from ports on both the northern and southern coasts of the big turtle-shaped island. Here they replenished supplies of water and dropped off or picked up cargo. In the late summer of 1942, the Japanese attempted to seize Milne Bay as one axis of a two-pronged attack on Papua. It was intended to be a base from which they'd cross the Owen Stanley Mountains and capture the heavily defended capital, Port Moresby. By decoding intercepted messages, however, Allied intelligence learned of their plans. Australians, with the aid of a small contingent of American combat engineers, seized Milne Bay, built an airstrip, and reinforced the base. This was one of the first land battles in the southwest Pacific and was strategically important in the Allies' master plan.

Our ship tied up to a dock less than a hundred feet from shore. Immediately there was a great bustle of activity as we took on water while sweaty, heavily tanned servicemen loaded and unloaded cargo. Inland, among the dust-laden vegetation, were the sheds, storehouses, and corrugated tin–roofed buildings of the military.

That night the promenade decks were lit and we had a dance aboard the ship. Although we were so close to shore that we could talk to GIs who had hurried to the dock to get a glimpse of women, we couldn't invite them aboard. Other than the crew and military stevedores, no one left or boarded the ship.

We were in the harbor at Milne Bay for two days and a night before we got under way and headed out to sea, paralleling but beyond the sight of the southeast coast of the island.

Oro Bay, Papua, New Guinea
November 2–9, 1944

Finally, on November 2, 1944, we bade farewell to the *Lurline*. We had pulled into the harbor of Oro Bay, near Buna, where New Guinea's bloodiest battles had been fought. Simultaneous with the attack on Milne Bay, the Japanese had seized Buna and were moving along the Kokoda Trail over the Owen Stanley Mountains toward Port Moresby. The Aussies headed them off on the ridge above the port and pushed them back to Buna, where the American 32d Division had landed. The terrible slaughter continued until the Japanese were driven out and northward along the coast. MacArthur was eager to use the area to prepare the way for the invasion of the Philippines. Buna fell in January 1943. The region was now secure.

We had no idea where Oro Bay was—it wasn't on the map in the New Guinea pocket guide. Neither did we know if the U.S. Army was fighting Japanese in the immediate vicinity. All we knew was that we were a thousand miles from Brisbane, where we had expected to work as code analysts at GHQ. Apparently the exigencies of the Leyte invasion necessitated sending us to the nearest WAC base in New Guinea. Because of our training and the importance of our work, we assumed that the army would eventually sort it out. Meanwhile, we were too excited about our landing to give the situation further thought.

After debarking we waited in the dock area for transportation to the WAC area, sited on a former Japanese base. The usual waterfront activity was made more exciting and colorful by the native "fuzzy-wuzzies." So named for the bushiness of their hair, they had acquired peroxide from the sailors and had bleached their hair and decorated it with combs and shredded purple packing paper. One approached me and asked to buy my Hobby hat—"I give you two florins." Still in a fascinated trance, and vaguely thinking I'd never be wearing dress uniform in this New Guinea jungle, I sold it.

We boarded "ducks," amphibious jeeps (designate DUKWs by the military), and drove on the beach road to the WAC area. Along the way, natives would shout, "Hubba, hubba!" a greeting I interpreted to be the equivalent of a wolf whistle. In minutes we covered the short distance, climbed out of the duck, and settled ourselves under a cluster of coconut palms while we waited for our bags and assignment to barracks.

The WAC area reminded me of a girls' summer camp. Five or six one-story buildings with corrugated tin roofs and burlap sides stood in a row close to the narrow strip of beach. Coconut palms grew on both sides of the path in front of the barracks and the road separating them from the beach.

The unenclosed compound area contained the usual orderly room and mess hall. Shower rooms were attached to the barracks; they were unroofed, for solar heating the water for the chain-pulled showers. There were several open-sided thatched buildings, one of which was a dance pavilion, and an unfinished thatched-roof army chapel. Near the mess hall stood a wigwam structure that held the Lister bag, a large canvas bag of chlorinated water with a spigot near the bottom. The palm trees didn't provide adequate shade, so the water was usually warm, and it tasted brackish. We preferred to wait until mealtime and drink "battery acid," a synthetic lemonade that was usually cool.

Overseas mess procedure was new to us. First, we had to be checked off the Atabrine list to be sure we'd taken the bitter little pill that dyed the skin yellow and served as a substitute for quinine, the malaria preventative. Before eating, the mess kit—with the knife, fork, and spoon looped over the handle—had to be dipped into a garbage-can-sized container of boiling water in order to sterilize it. After eating, leftovers were scraped into a garbage can, the mess kit and utensils were dipped into a can of soapy boiling water, scrubbed with a large brush similar to a toilet brush, and dipped into two more cans of rinsing water. The whole procedure was efficient.

We were assigned to cots equipped with mosquito nets suspended from wires that stretched the length of the barracks. Because we were not furnished with mattresses (or pillows), the nets had to be tucked carefully under the folded blankets that we used as a substitute pillow. The nets were also effective deterrents against rats, which we discovered during our first night at Oro Bay when we were awakened from a deep slumber by terrifying screams. None of us had any idea how close we were to the fighting or how near the Japanese might be. My first thought was they'd crept into our area and we were under attack. Instead, our nighttime intruders turned out to have four legs. The victims tucked their nets more tightly and resolved to endure.

The only other nightly distractions at Oro Bay were winds that lashed the fronds of the palms and loosened coconuts that fell on the roofs of our huts.

We were pleasantly surprised by the relaxed dress code of the small complement of Wacs stationed there. Almost anything seemed to be the uniform of the day as long as it was based on government issue, however altered. Hobby hats were modified in creative ways. Li'l Abners were cut down into serviceable and more feminine footwear—mainly sandals. Whenever possible, HBTs were replaced by suntan pants scrounged from the men, which fit better and were more suitable for the tropical heat. (We learned quickly that an important criterion for selecting a date was the size of his suntan pants.)

Most imaginative were the bathing suits made from scarves, straps, pieces of cloth, and other items procured from sailors and natives. With a tropical sandy beach so readily available, a bathing suit was a necessity.

I was eager to get to the beach the first night and fulfill my dreams of tropical paradise inspired by the song "South Sea Island Magic": "Do you recall our meeting, at a camp-fire that blazed near the ocean? . . . " There was no camp-fire blazing near the ocean, but there were palms and sand, and the coral reefs offshore gleamed in the moonlight.

During the day, we spent a lot of time on the beach, sunning, talking, looking for shells, and engaging in other aimless beach pastimes. Sunning was too hot for me, so I'd walk along the sand, picking up shells and poking around in the debris. Once I came upon a GI dog tag, a sobering reminder of the savage fighting that took place in the region. I thought it fitting to return it to the sand. What was he like? What would his family be thinking if they were standing here? Offshore a wrecked barge was another grim reminder of the war.

I enjoyed watching the natives as they were building the chapel or performing chores around the compound, such as stripping the fronds from the boles of palms and lashing them together for framework to support roof thatching. When one of them climbed a palm, we would watch him work his way down. Often they sang or chanted as they worked. Although they usually ignored us, one asked Margery Cady for the time in perfect English, and another snapped to attention when he saw her with a camera.

Just before we left Oro Bay, we were told to bring our overcoats, rubbers, and field jackets (ski pants and four-buckle overshoes not included) to the compound and turn them in, which meant throwing them on a huge pile. When asked what was going to be done with them, the Wac in charge said that they'd be burned. I especially loved my overcoat, and I deplored the horrible waste. But the army had its reasons. They were flying us up north soon and needed to cut down on the cargo. Space aboard the ship was equally at a premium. Why were they issued in the first place? we wondered. Later, someone reminded us that we were supposed to have gone to Australia.

We found out that we would soon be sent to Hollandia, Dutch New Guinea. After a week we were on our way along the dusty road to the Dobadura airstrip.

I was excited because this would be my first plane trip. We boarded a C-47 and took off to the north, following the shore for at least two hundred miles before turning inland at Lae. As I looked down at the lush mountains and valleys in varying shades of green, I thought if I brushed my hand over them they'd be as soft as moss. Once I saw a little village of thatched huts, the only sign of human habitation in all the vastness that stretched before me. A rainbow arched over an expanse of luxurious green. A narrow gray thread, the Sepik River, wound its way through the jungle as our plane droned toward Dutch territory. At last, dropping low over more mountains and valleys, we saw the harbor of Hollandia. The day had now deepened into night.

Six

Gleaming like a vast city lay a gigantic armada. Ships of every size, from battleships, cruisers, and destroyers to tugs and a variety of harbor craft, were assembled. All nations of the Pacific world were represented, packed so tightly they could barely maneuver, waiting to go north to support the Philippine invasion that was in progress. The surrounding darkness accentuated the profusion and motion of searchlights sweeping the sky, signal lights blinking messages back and forth, and countless tiny points of light moving about on the decks and along the shore. The spectacle was engrossing but disquieting, too, as I vaguely sensed the import of what was taking place.

We landed on the airstrip some thirty miles inland, at the base of Cyclops Mountain. The army transported us to a nearby mess hall for a meal and a rest stop. Shortly afterward, riding atop our duffel bags in a two-and-a-half-ton truck, we bumped back toward the harbor—thirty miles of chokingly dusty washboard road that had been hastily built after Dutch New Guinea was taken by the Allies. Finally, we reached the WAC compound at Base G.

The base, comprising harbor and dock installations, navy and army compounds and administrative buildings, a base hospital, and a WAC compound, spread out in all directions from the harbor. In April 1944 the Japanese were taken by surprise when the Americans attacked Hollandia. Expecting an invasion at Wewak, 250 miles south, they withdrew their main forces, leaving only disorganized service units to defend the region. In only six days of light skirmishing, the Americans captured the harbor and the airstrip. The damage, which was slight, had been cleared away long before our arrival.

Adjacent to the base was a stretch of beach, called Imbi, that had been set aside for recreational use. Imbi was everything a South Seas paradise should be: a wide strip of fine pale sand and slender coconut palms leaning gracefully toward a turquoise sea that shaded into aquamarine and, finally, into an intense midnight blue on the horizon. Unlike the beach at Oro Bay, which was littered with bits of coconut husks, dried fronds, and other debris, Imbi appeared fresh and clean, as if it had just been swept. From it extended a narrow red-dirt road that wound up a low hill to the WAC area, about a half mile away.

The land leveled off where the WAC compound stood, surrounded by a high chicken-wire fence and guarded by patrolling male MPs. The mess hall, rec hall, and orderly room stood apart from the tent area. Below that, on a little slope, were the showers and latrines.

We were dropped off with our duffel bags and escorted by a Wac to the area where we were assigned, six to a standard fifteen-foot-square tent. The tents were empty. In addition to dragging our duffel bags through the dirt to our respective tents, we had to go back to the orderly room, pick up our cots, take them back, and set them up before we could settle in. Setting up an army cot isn't easy; the canvas has to be stretched so the holes in the wooden end pieces will accommodate the knobs on the side ones. It had been a long day, and it was even longer before we got through at midnight. Such a vexing task performed by six people in limited space would normally strain tempers, but we went at it with humorous goodwill.

It was obvious immediately that our living conditions would be more primitive than any we had encountered so far. I didn't mind. There were no floors for the tents, and trenches had to be dug around them to keep the rain from turning the dirt into mud. The tents leaked, so we had to use our helmets and No. 10 cans to catch the drips. There was no electricity, but someone found candles, which were fine except we had no safe place to set them. There weren't any hooks or nails upon which to hang our clothes, which would mildew if left in the duffel bags without frequent airing. If shoes weren't dry by the time we went to bed at night, they'd be mildewed and still wet in the morning. I kept mine well polished, which helped. On the other hand, we never had to use the rat traps that someone had brought from Oro Bay, and we weren't bothered by insects other than flies. The showers had faucets and sprays rather than chains that dumped water straight down on our heads when we pulled them. And we had shower curtains. More modest than many, I liked that best of all.

We settled down in our little tent home, which we named "Hog Wallow." In no time, "family" members contributed packing boxes, nails, wire, wood, and other useful items that added a touch of domesticity.

Life was serene, except that we had nocturnal prowlers. Although the MPs were diligent, every now and then a GI would try to sneak in. It was unsafe to go to the latrines or showers without a partner, because there had been some incidents of rape. The Gremlin, or Gremmy, whose cot was next to the doorway, stretched a string across it, to which she attached tin cans. One night we were all sleeping soundly when suddenly a body landed on me, knocking my breath out with a whoosh. I was too frightened to scream, which was fortunate because it was only the Gremlin. She'd heard scuffling outside and had come over to get me. When the footsteps approached the tent she panicked and leaped. It turned out to be two of the cooks on their way to the mess hall to cook breakfast.

Living conditions at Base G may have been rugged, but opportunities for varied social activities more than compensated for any lack of comfort. Dating headed the list, and the opportunities were endless. There were at least 10,000 men to one woman at Hollandia, so responding to date invitations was a difficult choice.

At the compound gates the night after our arrival, crowds of GIs, sailors, and Aussies pushed against the chicken-wire fence, jostling to get our attention. They dangled beads, bracelets, pendants, and rings that they offered if only we'd come over and talk to them.

Many of the objects were lovely, especially those made from Australian coins. The silver in these was so pure and soft that it could be cut and hammered easily. For instance, rings were made by cutting a hole from the center of a shilling and tapping it with a mess-kit spoon, a process that was time-consuming but effective. I have a ring that is so carefully formed that the only indication of its origin is hidden on the inside.

Coins of various denominations were cut into strips and hammered into tiny links for coin bracelets. Sometimes the coin was hammered carefully over a rounded hard object, probably of carved wood, producing a convex contour that didn't deface the design or lettering on the coin.

I saw several heart-shaped pendants made of melted GI toothbrush handles and mounted with a cutout Liberty head dime. These were suspended from dog-tag chains, which could sometimes be purchased in the PX.

Our way of solving the problem of whom to date was by attending parties given by various outfits. This way we could dance, eat, talk, and have fun with as many as possible; if we met someone we really liked, we could accept a date for another time.

The fellows went to a lot of trouble getting food, tracking down a band, and decorating the mess halls, where the parties were usually held. Some of the decorations were innovative, because there weren't many materials at hand. The most popular material, because it was usually the most available, was toilet paper. It was made into pinwheels, rosettes and floral designs, and streamers, or twisted into festoons. Navy and Seabee parties were usually the best because they had good food, and the beer and drinks were always cold. I met a handsome but young sailor at one of these dances who was even more naive than I; we dated while I was at Base G.

During our three weeks at the base, the beach was our daytime hangout. We played bridge, laying the cards on a blanket in the sand. Occasional bystanders filled in as fourths when one or another of us was taking a swim. We became friends with a group we called the commandos. Their heads had been shaved as part of the equatorial rite of passage, and they were intentionally clowning around, which further attracted our attention. They were clever and likable, and the next thing we knew we were joining them in the fun. After that we'd meet them every day to play cards, swim, and go to the Red Cross canteen on the beach for the coffee and doughnuts that constituted lunch.

We tried never to go back to the detachment for lunch. The army was nervous about people remaining idle, so the NCOs would snag us for details. I was slow in catching on to this and was nailed for KP. Bell was nabbed at the same time. We were going about our tasks, one of which was cleaning the floor and tables and lining up the sugar bowls and salt and pepper shakers—a job that was taking us an inordinately long time. Bell decided to switch the salt and pepper at the officers' table, picturing Lieutenant Guild at the moment of discovery. Lieutenant Guild was a perfectly nice person as far as we knew—it was just that she looked as if she'd stepped off a classical vase. Bell, who liked poetry as well as I, was with me the first time we saw her, and I had remarked, "What maidens loth? What mad pursuit?" from Keats's "Ode on a Grecian Urn." Bell choked with laughter. After that, whenever we'd see Lieutenant Guild, one or the other of us would use the quote. No one else understood what was so hilarious.

The other detail for which I was "selected" before I wised up involved sweeping flies in the latrines after they'd been sprayed. New Guinea common house flies were large, and there were dustpans full of them.

The detail crew also lay in wait at breakfast time, so Bell and I would sneak out the gate just as the others were going to the mess hall. Halfway down the hill to the beach was a men's outfit where a line formed for breakfast. We'd slip in, have a meal—to which no one ever objected—and be on our way. Meanwhile, Marge, Gladys, or Bowman might be sweeping flies or deepening the rain trench around the mess hall.

In mid-November the rainy season began. The sun had

baked the earth so hard that when the downpours came little water soaked in and took some time to run off. We once walked through water up to our calves. Then the rain would stop suddenly, the sun would come out, and the cycle would begin again.

For purposes of morale, the army provided us with a festive Thanksgiving dinner—real turkey and gravy, fresh mashed potatoes, creamed onions, asparagus tips and corn (both canned), hot rolls, iced tea, canned fruit cocktail, and pumpkin pie. Considering the logistic problems of those times, it was an accomplishment.

Finally, we said good-bye to the lazy life at Base G and headed inland on the Queen Wilhelmina Highway to GHQ on the mountainside above Lake Sentani. This was the same road we'd taken the night of our arrival in New Guinea, but in the daylight we could enjoy the scenery as we jounced along. In places the highway, hemmed in by overhanging jungle, ran on the level. It then wound its way uphill and down, emerging for short stretches along the lake. Finally, it climbed a long hill. At the crest were the buildings of GHQ, MacArthur's advance headquarters, with a spectacular view.

We were now at least 2,000 feet above sea level overlooking Lake Sentani, silvery gray and dotted with rounded pale green islands. Rising high above us, on our right, was a great cloud-encircled mountain, giant Cyclops, presiding majestically over a tropic domain.

As we wound around the side of the mountain, we saw a tent village of Seabees nestled in a valley below us on our left. The road ended shortly, at the entrance to the WAC area. At last we were home. But for how long? Only the fortunes of war would decide that. At least we'd be doing what we'd come 10,000 miles to do, and we were eager to get started.

The WAC area was on a partially leveled-off section of mountainside above the lake. The entrance to the burlap and wire-fenced compound faced the mess and rec halls, behind which a path led about fifteen feet to the tent area below. There were eighty tents, and two sets of showers and latrines.

We were allowed to pick a tent, and there was a rush to grab one as close as possible to the end latrine. Proximity to toilets and showers was desirable because towels and articles of clean clothing, as well as our bodies, got wet in transit during the tremendous downpours of the rainy season. Sue, Jane, Bea, Juanita, "Slapsie Maxie" Clopine, and I ended up three tents away from the showers and latrines on the outside row. Had we had time to think about it, our choices in tent mates might have been different, but we were too preoccupied with choosing the tent. Two amenities were immediately obvious. We had a cement floor. And we had an electric light—only twenty-five watts for the whole tent, but better than candles.

While we waited for the army to discover our arrival, we set up housekeeping. Someone procured short lengths of board and wire with which we made storage shelves, nails for hanging up a few items of clothing, and a packing box that a G.I. readily traded for cigarettes. Covered with a GI towel, the packing box made a serviceable table, and a bouquet of wild orchids provided a domestic touch. We spread our uniforms and those items most likely to mildew on cots to dry in the sun, then we repacked and stored the barracks and duffel bags wherever we could stuff them. Helmets, gas masks, and musette bags were hung on supporting beams of the tent. Six of us and our cots in a fifteen-foot-square tent was cozy, but all was secure. Later, we decided to call our home "Secret Trash," a term referring to waste papers that we used in our signal intelligence work.

We were ordered to report for duty in the advance echelon of SIS (Signal Intelligence Service). SIS was a branch of Central Bureau (CB), an international bureau composed mainly of American and Australian signal intelligence units based in Brisbane, Australia. SIS, under the operational control of GHQ, was directed by Col. Abraham Sinkov. He was one of the three original disciples of the "father" of SIS, the brilliant William S. Friedman, who was appointed by the army to found and organize the service after the State Department closed the famous "Black Chamber" in 1929. The officers directly in charge of us and to whom we reported that first week in December were 1st Lt. Victor Rose and Lt. John R. Thomas.

Our office, one of three Quonset huts near the GHQ buildings, was ideally situated for work that required a quiet, relaxing atmosphere.

At that time, SIS, which included girls who had been trained before our arrival, was working on decoding one of the Japanese shipping codes. We were told that, in the haste of their departure from Midway, the Japanese hadn't burned the codebooks thoroughly or stirred the ashes, setting the stage for a valuable entry to be made into their code systems. Back at Vint Hill, we'd been thoroughly warned about the necessity of destroying all papers and scrap pieces that we'd been working on during the course of a shift, by burning them and carefully stirring the ashes. Despite the remote location of GHQ, this procedure was carried out every night, using a large oil drum that stood outside our Quonset.

It was our job to recover new values from messages to fill in gaps in the codebooks, then pass them, along with any pertinent information from the actual messages, to our superiors in signal intelligence. We'd been so well trained at Vint Hill that the transition was smooth despite the fact that we received little if any direction or supervision from our superiors. After preliminary explanations, we sat down at tables, spread out our papers, and went to work.

We knew little about the organization of SIS, but it worked something like this. Signal radio intelligence would intercept messages that the Japanese transmitted in an enciphered four-figure code and send them along to traffic analysis, where call signals and dates of transmission would be identified and analyzed. Somewhere along the line, the key words used to encipher the four-figure code would be determined, and the messages would be passed along to our cryptanalytic section. At that time the Japanese were using exotic names for key words, which they changed every month.

Each of us, or each pair if two were working together, would copy on a large sheet of paper a number of messages that used the same key word. Decoding with known values, we'd run through the messages until they yielded a sufficient amount of plain text to make sense. From the text of a given message we could often assume values for the unknown code words and test them against the texts of other messages to assure validity. We'd work until we either completed the messages or determined a sufficient amount of text to extract information and add values to the codebook.

The messages usually followed a set pattern—the call sign of the transmitting station, sets of numbers informing the receiver which code to use, and other necessary information. The text of the message ignored one of the great no-no's for the transmitter—the necessity of avoiding repetitive phrases. Typically, they began with the name of the ship, the time of departure, the nature of the cargo, and the expected time of arrival. Most textual material was boring to us but often informative to our superiors in G-2, who were eager to get information concerning frequency, concentration, and types of supply movements. However, I remember a message that told of a ship carrying an interesting cargo—women. Were they geishas? Whoever they were, they didn't rate the status of passengers.

I loved the work. I would lose all track of time pursuing the meaning of the messages, and it was exciting when things began to fall into place. I'd take a breather and pass a note to Bell or Gremmy, usually containing a cartoon, a pun on a Japanese word, or a line from a pop song we'd been trying to recall. They did likewise. Despite those frustrating times when we struggled to come up with something that made sense, we all took great satisfaction in doing the job we were trained to do and making a tangible contribution to the war effort.

At times the heat was oppressive. It increased slowly but intensely until by late morning it was extremely uncomfortable. Normally, I perspire very little, but by noon the back of my shirt would be drenched. Fortunately, at this latitude in the tropics, the mountains and higher elevations were often enshrouded with clouds and mist that offered relief.

Shortly after our arrival we were summoned for an orientation and introduction to the officers and noncoms of the U.S. Armed Forces in the Far East (USAFFE) WAC detachment, to which we were attached. One of the officers, from a rural area of the South, warned us about mosquitoes. After telling us how to identify the malaria-carrying anopheles (it bites with its proboscis at a right angle to the skin), she stressed the importance of keeping our sleeves down and buttoned at all times. At that moment, she scratched herself, retrieved a small box from her bosom, inserted the victim, and remarked, "Ah collects those little varmints."

The first sergeant, a talented honky-tonk singer and piano player, entertained us one evening. Especially memorable were her renditions of "Some of These Days" and "Won't You Come Home, Bill Bailey."

One of the officer replacements who arrived after we'd been there awhile decided to do something about "shaping up" the detachment, so the decree came down that there'd be regular inspections, everyone would stand reveille each morning, and the "appalling laxity" of the dress code would be tightened. Inspections and reveille were all but unenforceable, because people worked different shifts and slept at all hours, but the CO insisted. I remember a sergeant running from tent to tent begging sleeping recalcitrants to please fall out for reveille. Eventually, the officer in question was replaced by Lieutenant Toffaletti, whose only order was a Saturday morning inspection.

Mary "Ginny" Blakemore described my attire as "outlandish." To me it was strictly utilitarian—a pith safari helmet when it rained (I didn't like to struggle with the top of my poncho slipping down to my eyebrows), or a light, less cumbersome fatigue cap with white pajama strings. Like others, I cut off the tops of my Li'l Abners but kept them meticulously polished.

Life at the USAFFE WAC detachment settled into a routine. Except for rumors of transfers to other jobs, the thought of which petrified us, our chief concerns were the two most common to all in the overseas military: food and mail.

The food was monotonous and unappetizing. The army provided canned goods, dehydrated foods, bread, and occasionally real potatoes. The Australians shipped generous supplies of bully beef. For Christmas and Easter, we had fresh eggs. Once we were served cookies that had been stored near cans of gasoline. Bell declared that she was afraid to light a cigarette for fear of setting herself on fire.

Variety was achieved in name only by alternating the same items. For protein it was bully beef, Spam, dehydrated eggs, and cheese. Vegetables were beet greens, stewed tomatoes, canned carrots and peas, and dehydrated potatoes. Fruit cocktail and canned peaches provided vitamin C. Bread could be spread with "jungle butter," a runny margarine-like substance that didn't spoil in the heat. Because anything with chocolate melted in the heat, we had "equator bars," which required teeth like a beaver. I gnawed on one around the edges for weeks before I gave up and threw it away. Later, we were given Baby Ruth bars, Tootsie Rolls, sticky Aussie butterscotch, and Zagnuts, a poor imitation of a Butterfinger without the chocolate.

In early April our mess hall was closed and we were sent to another one at GHQ. The food there was no better. We supplemented our diet in any way we could, chiefly by attending parties given by the navy or Seabees, who were supplied with the best food on the island.

One day a scrawny chicken strayed into our area, creating ripples of excitement as it wandered along our row of tents. That night there was a bonfire on the hillside and the chicken was never seen again. Some of us thought that killing an emaciated chicken seemed barbaric and beneath the dignity of anyone in SIS.

Anyone who has been stationed overseas in wartime knows that mail call is an important event. Psychologically, receiving no mail is worse than unappetizing food. For those who stand around eagerly waiting for their names to be called, only to have stood in vain while others are happily tearing open envelopes and struggling with strings on packages, the occasion is grim. For nearly a month our group experienced this unhappy condition. Because we'd been moving around so much, previous mail was slow in catching up to us. To confuse matters further, our army post office numbers were changed three times within the first month even though we hadn't moved from our tents. It normally took two weeks to get a letter, longer for V-mail, which some said was faster, and two to three months to get a package. Packages had to be requested, except for birthday boxes, which had to be designated as such. Stories circulated about letters that were returned to the States and remailed a second time. One girl's brother got a Christmas package that had been mailed to him two years previously when he was in Iran. We listened to these tales apprehensively.

Finally, in mid-January, a spate of mail and packages began coming through. I got my Christmas goodies. It and a birthday package were the only ones I received while overseas. Although the Christmas cookies had crumbled and the hard candies had melted into sticky chunks, I ate them anyway. March was the worst month for mail, perhaps because of the invasion of Luzon, which had begun in February. There were only three or four letters a day for the whole camp, and morale hit an all-time low.

During the first six weeks we were at GHQ, we had trouble getting simple necessities such as soap, washcloths, towels, and facial tissue. Finally, in mid-January a PX was opened, but there was such a rush that the right to buy most of the items had to be raffled off. We relied mostly on packages from home and whatever we could procure from men in the various service outfits.

Day-to-day life on "the hill" was not always grim. As Christmas approached everyone got into the spirit. Someone ingeniously constructed a Christmas tree from branches of bushes gathered on the mountainside. Those who received cards cut out Santa Clauses, bells, and holly, which they contributed for tree decorations. Others saved scraps of string and colored paper for the tree and the mess hall, where the tree was installed. The men, too, were busy decorating for numerous parties, to which we were invited.

One clear night a reminder of the Christmas season came from an unexpected source. Far in the distance, down on Lake Sentani, the natives were singing "Silent Night" in perfect harmony. The voices of those simple people from the jungles of New Guinea, so far removed in time and place from the night in Bethlehem of which they sang, have lingered in my memory ever since.

Around this time, Jane and Sue met Bob and Chuck from the 161st Combat Photo Unit (Sig Photo), which was attached to the 1st Cavalry Division. The boys were on leave from the fighting at Leyte, in the Philippines. Jane and Sue accepted an invitation for lunch at their mess hall and swimming afterward at the CB pool. They asked me along as a date for Jim, who had received a "Dear John" letter from his wife and needed cheering up.

We had begun working the five to midnight shift and I'd been planning to relax that afternoon. I wasn't in the mood for amusing a disconsolate GI, I couldn't swim, I didn't have a swimsuit— I had lots of excuses. When Jane said she'd lend me her extra suit—in fact, she'd give it to me—I said okay and we went to the rec hall where they were waiting. I was introduced to a slim, dark-haired man in his late twenties. He seemed a little standoffish. In actuality he was shy and self-conscious because he suspected that I'd been told why he was brought along. However, it wasn't long before we were getting acquainted. I learned that he was a Greek American from Washington, D.C., and that he was a veterinarian in civilian life.

I had never been to the swimming hole before. To reach it we followed a path through the jungle and up a short distance to the mountainside, for the pool was a dammed-up section of a clear, freshwater mountain stream. The jungle trees stretched a hundred feet or more skyward in thick stands that filtered the sunlight. The diffused yellow-green light and the constant high-pitched singing of thousands of insects created an eerie world.

That was the first of many days off when we took picnic lunches and went to the swimming hole. Jim taught me to float and swim underwater, where he first kissed me. My swimming rapidly became more proficient beneath the water than above it.

Later, I made the mistake of telling Sue and Jane about the underwater kiss. They couldn't ignore a golden opportunity to rag me—saying it was my imagination and that it was just a passing guppy with big, fat lips. I remained deliriously unabashed.

Shortly after, a few Christmas packages began arriving, but not for me. When Jim heard of this, he came one evening with one of his to share. I was touched by his kindness, which was above and beyond the call of duty when it came to Christmas delicacies.

The day before Christmas, Irving Berlin came to our mess hall for lunch and presented a program of his favorite songs. He was there only briefly, but we were thrilled that he had given his precious time to our small group of Wacs.

On Christmas Eve someone built a bonfire on the hillside outside our Quonset and got the water boiling for our "tea" break. The night was beautiful and clear; we could see Lake Sentani shining like old silver. Clouds enshrouded the peak of Cyclops, and the sky was bright with stars. Despite the beauty of the night, our thoughts were far, far away as we sang the old, well-known carols. With moist eyes we went silently back to work.

After New Year's we knew that Sig Photo would be leaving soon to go "up north." We also knew what this meant, because they were combat photographers. Speculations regarding their destination were abundant.

Shortly before they left, we spent an evening at the Glid'er Inn. Built by engineers on a knoll near the airport, the inn was actually a large nightclub, roughly fifty to sixty feet square, constructed mostly of bamboo with a tin roof and a smoothed concrete floor for dancing. The ceiling was decorated with white, orange, and turquoise parachutes through which dim lights filtered. There were solidly built wooden tables and chairs, a bamboo decorated bar, and a platform for an orchestra that was composed of GI musicians from some of the best stateside bands. Outside was a lighted concrete patio with a view toward the jungle and a small stream.

The orchestra played favorite numbers, the beer was cold, the conversation was witty and stimulating, and the one I most wanted to be with was holding my hand under the table.

When it was time to leave, all of us clambered into the Sig Photo weapons carrier and began sliding our way home over "Slippery Willie," the Queen Wilhelmina Highway. Heavy rain made it difficult to see the edge of the road. Climbing a hill, we began slipping sideways down a gentle slope, catching on a boulder before going over a steep embankment. Extricating ourselves and discovering there were no injuries except for a few bumps and bruises, we slithered our way up to the road. The men flagged down a jeep with a couple of GIs who helped get our vehicle back on the road.

One night Jim came to the Quonset to say good-bye. Because he was going into combat, I had decided two things:

not to make any references to the future and not to get weepy. I managed pretty well with the first, but I just squeaked through on the tears. I felt that he was going to come through it and that I'd see him again. I did, but it was not to be for a long time.

One evening just after Jim left, I decided to go with some of the girls who regularly visited the wounded boys down in the naval base hospital. We went during what would be normal visiting hours in a hospital at home, but we were the only visitors. Two long rows of wounded from the Leyte campaign lay in their bandages and casts. Every now and then a tired-looking nurse hurried to attend to someone. Some of the men moaned or muttered to themselves; others were listless or quiet, either from sedation or depression. It was hot and muggy, unlike our mountainside location, which cooled off quickly at night, and the smell from the casts was fetid. When the men saw us, the alert ones called for us to come over and talk. One asked me to scratch his foot, which protruded from a long, heavy-looking cast. I talked to as many as I could, sometimes holding their hands if they asked. Many joked and kidded. I was more moved by their show of courage than by the suffering of the others. I left and was never able to make myself go back. Guilt over my cowardice haunted me for a long time.

Our chief medical problem was "jungle rot," a term that covered a wide spectrum of fungal infections. Sooner or later most of us got it, usually the mild variety that was treated with gentian violet. I got some between my fingers, which cleared up quickly, but Marge Wilhelm and Edith McMann had cases that required hospitalization. Marge broke out in sores all over her legs. Mac's was the most serious—the type that attacks the optic nerve and causes blindness—and she had to be shipped home. We learned later that she lost 90 percent of her vision.

Dental work wasn't much fun. After one occasion I vowed I'd let every tooth disintegrate before I'd go again; I submitted myself for replacement of two large fillings in my front teeth. The dentist had set up his foot-pedal drill and a straight-backed armless chair in the shade outside a tent. As soon as I sat down he began work, without an anesthetic. There was nothing to do but clutch my legs and endure.

I didn't worry about malaria because I took Atabrine faithfully. The combination of Atabrine with the tropic sun produced a golden suntan that faded to plain yellow after we were no longer exposed to the sun. I arrived home in winter and looked pretty ghastly for a month or two. The soles of my feet were last to fade, about five months later.

One day in late February, I went to see if a letter had arrived from Jim. Instead there was a card from Friendship. On my way down to the tent I opened it and discovered signatures from my school kids all over a sympathy card. At first I was puzzled. Then a cold fear swept through me. I reached the door of my tent and commented about the card. Marion came over and said, "It's your mother, Irene."

Marion's mother, who lived about ten miles from my parents, had learned of my mother's death from our neighbor and written to Marion. The girls had decided not to say anything but to let the Red Cross notify me. They left me then and went to lunch. I was devastated. Not only was I bereft of my mother, to whom I felt closer than anyone and could no longer turn to for support, but I was 10,000 miles from my sisters, whom I desperately needed for solace.

I stayed in the tent that afternoon and lay on my cot and cried. I thought of how I'd never see Mom again—see her twinkly blue eyes crinkle as she smiled, see the stray wisps of hair she tried to keep curled with a curling iron. Nor would I hear her whistling softly between her teeth as she went about in her apron with the flour on it. Although the manner in which I'd been notified left me feeling suspended in a void—I knew nothing of the circumstances of her death—I was glad I could remember her the way I last saw her rather than in a coffin. It was days later that one of my sisters wrote that my mother had died of an infection from a strangulated intestine.

Sue Cross, one of my best
friends in the S.I.S. "family."

Washington, D.C., July
1944. At that time ties were
not to be tucked in.

Jane receives the Soldier's Medal for heroism. Fort Myer, Virginia, July 25, 1944.

Margie and Gremmy, the twin perils of the S.I.S. "family."

"Bell," a great pal, with a penchant for attracting incident.

Me, Ginny, and Gremmy taking in our new tropical paradise at Or Bay, New Guinea.

Me, Ginny, and Gremmy waiting for assignment to barracks.

WAC barracks on the beach at Oro Bay.

Cady, Gladys, Marge, Betty, Marion, Bea, and I ready to trade our cigarette rations. Base "G," Hollandia, Dutch New Guinea, 1944.

Our first homes on the mountainside at GHQ, Hollandia. December 1944.

WAC detachment, Hollandia, 1944, with Lake Sentani in the background 2,000 feet below.

Signal Intelligence offices, GHQ, Hollandia. We worked in the middle quonset.

Advance Echelon of GHQ, Hollandia.

Cady and her
Christmas tree.

Jim, one of the Signal Corps photographers. We had several swimming and party dates.

At the Glid'er Inn, Hollandia. A memorable evening with an exciting ending.

Sue and I on a damp day after the usual gourmet lunch at the mess hall.

Gremmy, Margie, Bell, and I nattily attired in the uniform of the day.

Vi and Mac, shortly before Mac returned to the states with a serious fungus infection.

Mom.

Seven

About six weeks later I got a phone call from the Red Cross when I was at work. It was a telegram saying that my sister Mary had died. I thought they meant Marie. I was numb. They called back that afternoon and apologized, saying that they'd made a mistake. I never found out what happened. I assumed they had mixed up the telegram about Mom that the family had sent, probably with one for somebody else who had a sister named Mary. Or, more likely, it was Marie who notified them and the message was garbled in transmission.

One evening, shortly after the news about Mom's death, we were playing bridge when we were told to put on our helmets, prepare for a bombing attack, and await further instructions. We put on the helmets and continued playing cards. Everyone was calm. I was curiously excited but not frightened. We continued our game until the all-clear sounded, then ran out of the tent to find out what had happened. The Japanese had probably intended to bomb the airstrip and maybe drop a few on GHQ while they were at it, but they were driven back by units of our air force on Biak, an island about seventy-five miles off the New Guinea coast. Tokyo Rose had announced earlier that the Japanese were going to bomb the skirts off the Wacs at Hollandia.

Meantime I'd received some letters from Jim. He sent me Japanese invasion money that he got when they raided the Japanese finance office in Manila. Supposedly, the boys were rambling around the city in a tank when they came upon the semi-ruined building. The teller, who was also supposed to be a guard, had stepped out, so the boys waited on themselves. The invasion money, a hundred notes to a bundle, was printed for use in the countries Japan intended to occupy: pesos for the Philippines, guilders for the Netherlands East Indies, pound notes for Australia and New Zealand, rupees for India, and dollars for the United States, Hawaii, and Alaska. The notes indicated that "The Japanese Government Promises to Pay the Bearer on Demand. . . ."

Later, when I went to Manila, small-denomination notes were scattered everywhere in the central part of the city. People stepped on them; if there was a breeze, they fluttered about; if it rained, they clung limply to whatever debris lay where they'd fallen. Even eighty miles north, at San Miguel, I spotted a note on which someone had written: "In Memory of our Wedding. 7/17/43, Mesantol Catholic Church, Mas, Pamp," "God Bless Us Thee," "In God We Trust," and especially poignant, "God Help Us."

In addition to the invasion money, Jim included several sheets of stamps he picked up when his outfit took the Manila post office. Some of these were U.S. postage stamps that had been surcharged for use in the Philippines.

Like every GI, we were hungry for souvenirs. Besides the invasion money and stamps, I acquired fabric from downed Zeros and a few small cardboard boxes of Japanese officers' cigarettes. Bell sent her mother some of the cigarettes. She and her bridge friends smoked them, and Mrs. Bell wrote back, "Not too bad. Can you get any more?" Others acquired an occasional flag, knife, or bayonet, but it was Bea Hart who came up with the prize—a complete Japanese enlisted man's (EM) uniform, cap and all. She wore it to work frequently. No one attempted to stop her—not even a nervous GI with a gun.

We continued to go to the swimming hole on our days off, but it was never the same after Jim and his buddies left. Jane talked me into going on a picnic with one of her admirers, someone named Charlie, who bent my ear with his sad story of Jane's rejection and then proceeded to pounce on me. I had been dreaming nostalgically of happier hours spent there, so the date was not an outstanding success.

On another occasion I was watching a GI collect beer cans farther up the creek and set them up on the other side. When I approached him to ask what he was doing, I noticed that he had a small machine gun. He was friendly, explained how each part worked, and let me share target practice with him. The gun was a Reising, of German manufacture and deadly for its size. The experience was simultaneously exciting and chilling.

The biggest sport at the swimming hole was trying to catch the character who was stealing our GI panties out of the dressing tent. No money or other items, not even bras, disappeared, just the panties. Why someone would risk a court-martial to obtain these items was difficult to fathom, for they were not attractive. I was particularly upset because, to avoid mixups at the laundry, I had marked mine with "BRION" in big capitals across the front. I could just see a GI exhibiting them in his tent while he and his buddies laughed over details of his supposed exploits. We guarded the tent, but no one ever caught the culprit.

Sometime before Easter I met a GI who invited me to go with him to a native village in a mangrove swamp near the lake. We had to leave the jeep and walk the rest of the way. He had never been to the village, so he wasn't prepared for the thick vegetation of the swamp. In the drier areas we hacked our way through the tangled underbrush; when we reached the patches of swamp, he cut long hanging vines and we swung across like Tarzan and Jane. Once I didn't swing far enough and was left dangling in midair. He rescued me by swinging a vine, which I caught between my feet so he could pull me the rest of the way. In an hour we had covered only about a hundred feet, so we never made it to the village. That was our only date. He was transferred a few days later, much to my chagrin, for he was intelligent, polite, and kind.

On April 6 we had to move down to the last row of tents on the lower side of the compound. As more USAFFE girls, who made up the greater part of the detachment, were moved up to the Philippines, it was practical to consolidate those who remained. Now we were less crowded, with only three others in the tent with me: Sue, Jane, and Harriott Bell. We had room for our box table, more shelves, and a chair that someone procured. I scrounged around and found an orange crate, which came in handy as a cotside stand. On its top I set up pictures of Mom, Bugs Bunny (our mascot at Camp Carson), and Brion, my first nephew. On the shelf I put my prize possession, a tiny bottle of French perfume, Schiaparelli's Shocking, which I had bought when I was at Camp Carson. All was fine, except a black widow spider built a nest between the crate and the tent frame. I watched him carefully for a while and assumed he was a bachelor, as no babies arrived. He was so lazy that he didn't bother me, but I shook out my shoes and clothes each morning, just in case.

Other than flies, mosquitoes, and the sluggish black widows, I saw little animal life in our area. However, one night I was awakened by activity near my cot and, looking through my net, saw a small animal sitting on its haunches. Then it hopped out of the corner of the tent. I said it was a wallaby, but no one believed me; they insisted it was either a rat or a hallucination.

Another time we were sitting around talking when a tarantula appeared. Bea Hart grabbed a field shoe and swatted at it. The shoe struck just where the spider had been, so she repeated the action a couple of times, but each time the spider was literally one jump ahead of her. It was the fastest I'd ever seen Bea move. To our relief, it took off to the next tent. Soon we heard squeals and screeches, then silence. Then more squeals, diminishing in volume as the spider apparently made its way up the row of tents.

The most traumatic incident of all occurred, fortunately, when I was elsewhere. One noon a python was seen going into one of the tents, but by the time the girls took an apprehensive look, it wasn't in sight. They assumed that it had gone through. The girl who occupied the tent in question arrived shortly thereafter and discovered the snake coiled around part of the tent frame. Her screams incited further screaming and brought the MPs running. They knocked it down and the chase was on until they finally killed it. The python, which I saw later, was about five feet long, and the only snake I ever saw in New Guinea.

I didn't let the incidents trouble me. My thoughts turned to a recurrent theme—fresh vegetables—preferably green and crunchy. I had long given up on anyone sending me a package, so I requested something that could be mailed in an ordinary envelope, namely a package of lettuce seeds. Sue had received a can of tuna, which she was hoarding and agreed to share with me when I harvested my lettuce. We had our taste buds set for a tuna sandwich. The seeds came and I planted them outside my tent. The next day they were peeping through the soil, and by the third day there were lovely green leaves over an inch high. We were elated and salivated in anticipation. We decided to let them grow higher. A week passed with no evidence of a size increase. We waited a little longer, watering them carefully because they had begun to look listless. Finally, we pulled them out carefully by the roots, washed them, consumed our sandwich, and abandoned our dreams of further gardening.

One night an altercation arose between Cady and Ginny. Partially, at least, it was triggered by Ginny's having dumped out her beer ration rather than donating it to the boys at the hospital, as someone suggested she do. She made frequent trips to the hospital to help the boys, she had said, but her ministrations didn't include supplying them with sinful alcoholic beverages. Cady told her she was a hypocrite. Ginny came right back with the prediction that Cady was going straight to hell. One of their tent mates, who had been siding with Cady, wanted to know if she had her information straight from Jesus or if it had come through channels. It took a while before that was settled.

As Easter approached Sue talked me into going with her to the Seabee chapel. It was a charming thatched roof and bamboo building with a square tower, topped by a pyramidal bamboo structure that supported the cross. A small flight of steps led to the entrance. The chapel was unique because it had a wooden floor. There was no view of the lake, but the mountain setting had its particular ambience. Mount Cyclops, with ever-present clouds wrapped around its shoulders, towered close by, drawing the eye upward and evoking feelings of awe at the spirituality inherent in the natural world.

A domestic crisis of sorts occurred shortly after Easter. One of the USAFFE girls had brought up a young cat from Australia. Pussy had been indiscreet in Brisbane and gotten herself pregnant; she had gone into labor and couldn't give birth to the first kitten. The cat suffered all morning with the kitten half emerged. Her owner consulted me; she was told I had been raised on a farm and could probably handle the situation. I went to the darkened tent where the cat lay on a cot while the owner and her tent mates were anxiously awaiting any possible instructions from me. Belying my ignorance of veterinary obstetrics, I set to work, massaging the stomach and pulling on the kitten, but I couldn't get it out. Just then Sue came along and succeeded in extracting it. The kitten was dead of course, but shortly afterward a healthy gray one was born. Later that afternoon two black ones arrived, both in fine shape. In the near future, they were to accompany their mistress to the Philippines.

Later that spring, my veterinarian proficiency again failed me. A small, wiry-haired black dog wandered into our tent area. Like the chicken, it had probably come from one of the native villages a considerable distance away. It was scraggly and scrawny, with a pathetic little face. Bell and I immediately took it into our care, cleaning it up and feeding it. We named her Mary Ann. She didn't respond to our anxious attentions, and we knew she had to have professional help. We tracked down a veterinary outfit through sailors Bell knew, and they promised to take us there. The four of us and Mary Ann climbed into their jeep and drove almost to Base G before we found the vets. We carried the dog in while the men waited. Taking one look at her, the vet shook his head and, enumerating all that was wrong with her, said that the humane thing was to put her to sleep. Bell broke down completely and I was struggling with tears as we returned to the waiting sailors. They had brought along beer and food, expecting to have a lakeside party on the way home, but two sniffling and weeping females were hardly ideal dates for a picnic.

Bell had met some Aussies who were lots of fun and well supplied with Foster's ale, the kind that was bottled, wrapped individually in straw, and packed in wooden cases. We decided to accept their invitation to go on a picnic. There were several of them, so we brought along as many girls as we could. What names the boys had: Cookie, Nipper, Bluey (a redhead), and Major Curlilewis, who had taken off his pips and come along for the fun.

We sang songs that were familiar to all of us. They taught us "Waltzing Matilda" and a bawdy number sung to the tune of "Oh, Dear, What Can the Matter Be?" Using the first line, they added "Three old lydies locked in a lavatry. They were there from Monday 'til Saturday and nobody knew they were there." Then followed the names of the three old ladies, all named Elizabeth but having different surnames. Rhyming with the surname was the chief difficulty each encountered while in the water closet.

After that we often partied and traded American items for Aussie ones, which we were eager to get because of their superior quality. The Aussies were most interested in Montgomery Ward catalogs, but we never managed to get them. I acquired what I'd always wanted, a "digger" hat with insignia, and one of their lovely gray woolen blankets.

One of the Aussies was actually a Tasmanian, Ernie Lette, and I went out with him a few times. Army regulations required that escorts of Wacs in combat zones must sign up two days in advance of a date. They had to give name, rank, serial number, and organization, in triplicate. They also had to have a vehicle and carry a side arm. Passing through a main gate and a second gate, where their dog tags had to be shown, they finally arrived at the gate to the WAC compound.

Ernie came for me one night in a five-ton truck. I wasn't surprised when I saw the lorry in the parking lot because the lot always had a variety of vehicles: jeeps, weapons carriers, trucks, command cars, or occasionally an amphibious jeep. Once I even saw a road grader, which was the last resort of a determined suitor. What was strange was to ride in such a huge vehicle with my date sitting on the right-hand side.

Although social activities usually involved drinking, I saw little drunkenness while I was in New Guinea. Beer was the most common drink. The ration of one case a month was usually exhausted quickly, so GIs augmented their supply by trading, bribing, or hijacking. Once, a couple of us were en route to a party with two GIs whom the outfit had designated to pick us up. It was raining heavily, the road was slippery, and it was difficult to see. Suddenly, ahead of us, chugging slowly up a hill, was a two-and-a-half-ton truck loaded with cases of beer. Our driver turned off the lights and drew up close behind the truck while the other fellow edged his way carefully out onto the hood. From there he climbed onto the truck, threw off a couple of cases, and jumped down. That was one way to hijack.

Few army personnel had access to refrigeration, so beer was drunk warm. In the tropics the cans had to be opened carefully or the beer would shoot out and precious amounts would be lost. It was a fairly common sight to see someone rushing from her tent with a streaming, foaming can. I learned how to open cans of all kinds with my trench knife—we had no can openers. I held the can between my feet and gently made a very tiny hole with the point of the knife, allowing a minimum amount of air to get in before widening the hole. Even that wasn't always reliable.

Whiskey, both stateside and Australian brands, was rare and the prices were exorbitant, so those who wanted something stronger than beer resorted to dispensary alcohol, which they cut with water or battery acid. I tried some once at a picnic down at the lake. Someone had brought along treasured cans of grapefruit slices to which he'd added the alcohol. I discovered the fruit slices to be quite tasty and, forgetting the oppressive midafternoon tropic sun, partook of them generously. Later when some of us shoved off in a hollowed-out wooden native canoe to explore a nearby island, I leaned too far over the edge and fell out.

The desperate types built stills and made their own potables, chief of which was "raisin jack." A whole shipment of raisins that never reached its legal destination was brewed and consumed by the men. Although not as dangerous as "rotgut" whiskey, which caused numerous deaths, it probably contributed to cases of blindness among those foolhardy enough to drink it.

Besides the rounds of picnics and dance parties, movies were a popular form of entertainment. Unlike the mail, they arrived from the States with surprising promptness, so we saw many of the new releases. These included "Arsenic and Old Lace," "When Irish Eyes Are Smiling" with Dick Haymes, and Bob Hope in "The Princess and the Pirate." If it was raining heavily we saw the movies in our own rec hall, where they were shown three times a week. The rain sometimes created havoc with the generator's electrical output. I remember spending a whole evening trying to see Humphrey Bogart and Lauren Bacall in "To Have or Have Not" because the machine kept breaking down. The sound, too, was affected so that the voices were about an octave lower than normal. Because Lauren Bacall's voice was already low and husky, the love scenes were riotous.

The outdoor theater, located in a low natural amphitheater, was the main theater that everyone usually attended. Behind the wings on each side of the screen were two dressing rooms for United Service Organizations (USO) shows, and among the seats down by the apron of the stage was a projection booth. There weren't many seats, so the overflow sat on the ground of the surrounding slope. In case we were part of the overflow, we carried blankets to sit on and ponchos to put over our heads if it rained. At 1900 the news that had come in that day via teletype was read over the PA system by the man in the projection booth. Following this was the main feature, which usually ended by 2130, giving us ample time to get back to our area for check-in. Once in a while the MPs quietly whisked away a Japanese who had come down from the hills and crept into the audience. To him, a chance for entertainment was worth the risk.

In early April, right after Easter, SIS moved us out of the Quonset to one of the GHQ buildings farther up the hill. It was just like them to do that when we'd finally managed to negotiate the path down to the latrine. We were working with a number of men in a long building filled with plywood-topped work tables, which we appreciated after the crude, wiggly tops of those in the Quonset. The GHQ building may have been used as a barracks, because wires of the type used to fasten mosquito nets stretched the length of the structure.

One of the men working near me was an ardent southerner named Smitty; he had hung a Confederate flag from the wire over his table. When kidded about it he staunchly defended the flag, the cause, and the land of Dixie. Remembering a certain page in my history book at Freewill Number 8, I decided to make a placard and hang it beside his flag before he came to work. I went in early the next morning and hung my sign which read:

No terms except an immediate and unconditional surrender will be accepted.
Ulysses S. Grant
General, U.S. Army
Commanding

Those who arrived ahead of Smitty waited with me to see his reaction. For a moment he was visibly upset, then he gained control, smiled weakly, and tore up the sign. He never attempted to identify the perpetrator.

A few days after our office moved to the GHQ area, Franklin Roosevelt died. To pay him tribute, we ceased work at eleven the next morning and sat in silence for a minute. Although he looked older and thinner in newsreels we'd seen in the States, I don't think anyone realized how ill he had been. Most were saddened by his death and concerned about Truman's ability to conduct the war.

General headquarters in Hollandia had been MacArthur's headquarters when he was conducting operations from New Guinea. GIs passed along numerous stories about his luxurious million-dollar "mansion." The structure consisted of two mess halls that had been pulled together. They were already falling apart, and all that remained of his supposed extravagant lifestyle was a hardwood floor and a flush toilet. One of the carpenters who helped build MacArthur's house said he could build one like it anytime for five hundred dollars.

Although the general was now busy in the Philippines, he made at least one trip to New Guinea. Margie Morris was walking along the road one day when she saw a jeep approaching. As it drew near, she saw stars on the license plate and immediately snapped to attention. As she stood, holding her best salute, the jeep stopped for a second and MacArthur said, "That isn't necessary, little Wac." Then he drove off.

Margie, who had always been impressed by any brass of field rank, was ecstatic. We learned later that MacArthur not only liked Wacs but had insisted upon having us in his theater. In a report to General Marshall of an interview he had with the director of the WAC, Colonel Boyce, on October 14, 1945, he referred to the Wacs as "my best soldiers" and stated that they worked harder than the men, complained less, and were better disciplined. He also remarked that he'd take any number of Wacs the War Department would give him in any future command he might ever have. After Margie's experience he was our hero.

When we moved from the Quonset to the big office at GHQ, we still lived at the WAC detachment but had to take our meals in the men's mess hall, where the food was even worse and the climb up a steep hill exhausting. The officers had a roped-off section with tables set with plates, cups, and saucers, which we resented. The men and women vehemently objected to serving them.

During the last two months in New Guinea, our social life continued to be active. On one occasion Margie, who knew some air force pilots, easily talked them into giving her, Bell, and me a ride in a B-24 Liberator bomber. They took us out over Humboldt Bay and did a few tricks while I was back in the tail gunner's seat. I don't think the B-24, which was a heavy plane and the longest range bomber in the air force, was intended for such maneuvers. I know I wasn't, because I was green on top of my Atabrine tan. Still, the experience left me with a fuller appreciation of the air corps fliers and a special feeling for the big twin-tailed plane.

The Gremlin knew some air corps GIs who took us to a native village in the mountains above the airstrip. We picked our way over a narrow, rutted road that ran along the edge of a steep embankment. Suddenly we heard a high-pitched squealing and fifteen to twenty naked boys and girls burst over the edge of the ravine where they'd been playing. Some climbed onto the hood of the jeep; others just ran along screeching. One little fellow who had fallen down was crying, holding his backside, and trying to keep up. The children followed us the rest of the way.

The village was really a small settlement of a few thatched huts, one pleasant thatched house, and a schoolhouse, all of which surrounded an open square. The headman, followed by a varied retinue of women and children, came out to barter. The men and boys wore skirtlike garments that they wrapped around their waists and supported with a rolled band of cloth that served as a belt. The women, whose teeth were a brilliant deep pink from chewing betel nuts or berries used for dyeing, covered most of their bodies with a loose, dirty-looking garment. All wanted cigarettes and gum. "Cigarette, Joe?" "Cigarette, Mary?" All GIs were Joes or Marys. Assuming that the driver and I were married, one native asked me, "You his Mary?" The Gremlin and I had taken along paper clips and safety pins, which the natives were eager to have for earrings. They fastened them together so that they dangled decoratively. The longer the strands, presumably, the greater the prestige of the possessor.

Three or four young boys who were cleaner than the others spoke a little English and proudly told me, "No cigarette. We go school." They took me to the school, which proved to be the highlight of the trip. Of typical bamboo construction, it had a thatched roof and a porticoed entrance. Inside were benches and, in the front of the room, the Dutch missionary teacher's desk. On it was a small stack of slates like those used in rural schools in the United States as late as the early twentieth century. To my surprise, the top slate contained simple algebra problems. Around the walls were crayon drawings that the students had made of tropical fruits and objects familiar to them. Each was labeled in Dutch and the native dialect.

During those last weeks in Hollandia, some sailors took a couple of us on an unforgettable picnic. We went with them by jeep over the highway to the harbor of Humboldt Bay, where they were based. Leaving the jeep, we boarded a small landing craft and shoved off, following the coast toward Tanahmerah Bay. It was a beautiful night with a full moon, calm water, and a palm-fringed shore a short distance off our port side. We rounded a slight promontory and came upon a lovely cove with a thick stand of palms and a wide strip of sand, snow white in the moonlight. Drawing close to the beach, the boys let down the end of the boat and we rushed ashore, simulating an amphibious landing on a Japanese-held island. Under pretended fire, we carried the food and beer ashore, whereupon the casualties resurrected themselves in time to feast on ham and a special delicacy, a large jar of olives.

Eventually we tired of the same old round of parties and began staying in our tents more often. On rainy nights, especially, Gremmy and Bell would drop by and we'd sing popular songs, mostly oldies because we were months behind on the hits at home. One of us got the idea of writing the lyrics on slips of paper and putting them in a cardboard box. When we'd wonder what to sing next, we'd pull a slip out of the box. Not only could we enjoy the element of surprise, but the words were handy for anyone who had forgotten or didn't know them. We had quite a collection.

I acquired a ukulele, and the songfests evolved into a Spike Jones orchestra, complete with a ukulele, combs and paper, a washboard, and an ocarina. Our magnum opus was "Der Fuehrer's Face," a combination of solo, chorus, and orchestra. Bell, whose imitation of a German accent was flawless, took the solo part: "Iss diss Nazi land zo goot? Ve vould leaf it if ve could. Yah, diss Nazi land iz goot, ve vould leaf it if ve could."

We also had literary evenings when we read poetry or selections from the better overseas editions of well-known books. These mini editions were among the first American paperback books. Someone had a copy of Van Doren's *An Anthology of World Poetry*. We preferred British poetry, but I remember reading and rereading, aloud, Poe's "The Bells" and E. A. Robinson's "Miniver Cheevy." Popular, too, were the poems of Ogden Nash, then currently in vogue back home. Inspired, probably out of envy of those who received letters, I composed the following bit of doggerel:

> Of all the things that give me the jitters
> Are people who go around reading their litters
> And forcing me to pay attention
> To things that are almost as remote as Tientsin.
> It pains me and bores me to have to listen
> When there isn't any particularly good risson,
> To the progress and growth of auntie's zinnia,
> Or, "How do you like it out in New Ginnia?"
> So why can't people read them in silence?
> There'd probably be a lot less vilence.

There were several English literature majors in SIS, and they would drop by from time to time and join in or just listen. Our favorite prose selections were from James Stephens's *The Crock of Gold*, which provided considerable enjoyment and discussion. We read and reread it, and used some of the pithy Irish expressions in our daily conversation.

Some of us discovered that Wacs were sometimes taken along as sight-seeing passengers on Sunday afternoon mapping and reconnaissance flights over the interior of the island. Before we figured out how to get ourselves invited, an incident occurred that caused an immediate change in our plans. One Sunday in the middle of May, a C-47 carrying seven Wacs and fourteen air force men on one of the reconnaissance flights crashed into a mountain above Hidden Valley, an uncharted area of Dutch New Guinea. Five survived, three Wacs and two airmen, but two of the Wacs died during the night. Corporal Margaret Hastings and the two men, though badly burned, managed to get down the mountain, where they were met by fierce-looking natives bearing clubs and stone axes. Despite their formidable appearance, the natives proved to be friendly and took the three survivors to their village, where they fed them and attempted to treat their injuries.

Meanwhile, the search was on. After two or three days, the air force spotted signals that the survivors had laid out on the valley floor. Food, medicine, and clothing were dropped, but the enclosing mountains precluded landing a plane. The only solution to getting them out was by glider. Paratroopers assembled the glider and prepared an airstrip for the rescue operation. Two of the paratroopers were medical technicians. Expediency was imperative because Corporal Hastings's wounds were becoming gangrenous and she was in danger of losing her legs.

At Hollandia, we kept our fingers crossed while waiting for the daily news bulletins. Even though everyone was concerned about the success of the operation, to us there was special immediacy because Hastings was a fellow Wac.

Finally, after forty-five days, the glider was ready. The natives, who had become fond of their charges, stood weeping at the takeoff. During the hour-and-a-half ride back to Hollandia, a tiny rip in the fabric of the glider began to develop into a hole, but the party landed safely.

The two courageous pilots, who had to make two additional trips that were considered impossible in order to bring back the remaining personnel, were awarded the Distinguished Flying Cross.

Corporal Hastings's story, written after the war, appeared in the November 1945 issue of *Reader's Digest.* Few true-life stories could make a more exciting movie than the ordeal of Margaret Hastings.

By now the rains were intermittent, but when they did come along every few weeks they virtually deluged us. From the mountainside we could see the storms bearing down on us in great wind-driven sheets that obscured all behind them—Mt. Cyclops, the range beyond and the lake below. The tent developed new drips that necessitated everyone shifting her cot and putting buckets, helmets, or cans under the leaks. If drips developed over our mosquito nets, however, we had a problem. We used raincoats and ponchos to prevent steady drops of water on our faces, but the water accumulated in little puddles that soon grew heavy enough to spill over and drench us. There was nothing to do but to move our cots again.

After the storm passed, we would put our cots back, laughing as we quoted in unison from a *Saturday Evening Post* advertisement that I'd posted in my corner:

TELL-TALE TRACKS

Beware of that unsightly, washed out trough around the foundation of your house. . . . Chase Copper gutters and downspouts will carry away the rain-water from your roof and save your flower beds. . . . Sturdy, handsome, rust-proof Chase Copper gutters will improve the appearance of your house and last and last as only copper does.

During April and May, USAFFE had been making preparations to move to the Philippines. They sent some of their Wacs by ship, and in early June the last ones left by plane. One of the planes was rumored to have gone down, as a result of engine failure or Japanese attack. Even though we tried to assure ourselves that it wasn't true, we were shaken by the supposed loss of the girls. It occurred to us that we could suffer the same fate and suddenly the war came a little closer. We never found out if the rumor was true.

Before the dust of USAFFE's departure settled, a couple of us raided the trash cans, which were loaded with useful items that couldn't be taken on the plane. Apparently, while Bell and I were engaged in this absorbing activity, we missed hearing the news that leftover cans of food were being given away in the storeroom. We heard that everyone was grabbing the huge No. 10 cans, regardless of their contents. People were emerging with armloads of peaches, catsup, applesauce, synthetic lemon juice powder, sour cherries, and even Spam. Gladys triumphantly acquired condensed milk and instant coffee. One lucky soul made off with a can of peanut butter.

When someone realized at the last moment that the canvas roofs of the tents were on their inventory, USAFFE sent a party back to take them. They made no allowances for the fact that our small contingent was not going with them. All they left were the frames and the burlap sidings. Our CO called us to leave work and come home immediately to batten down our belongings with ponchos in case of rain while she searched the island for a QM that would lend her some tops. Fortunately, she succeeded. We returned to work, and by nightfall we had roofs over our heads.

When we were with USAFFE, we had laundry service. We merely put our dirty clothes in a bag and attached a list of what it contained. These would be checked off and the list returned. I saved one of the lists on which some wag had jotted down the following comments: "I bet you look cute in skirts." "My, my, what a thrill just thinking of these!" "Sure would like to keep these for encouragement!" I'd penciled out the comments until they were barely legible. Had I been angry? Embarrassed? Insulted? If so, why had I saved the slip? It's likely that I was secretly flattered.

Now that the laundry service was terminated, we made more use of our own laundry room, which was in the same building as our latrine and showers. It contained tubs, washboards, irons and ironing boards, and an old-fashioned hand wringer.

The only irons were Australian, nearly a foot long and heavy. They resembled battleships, and to me, equalled them in tonage. We used them for a few dress shirts, but otherwise we pressed things by folding them carefully, putting them under the folded blanket that served as a mattress, and sleeping on them.

At one point, Jane, Bell, and I decided to wash our clothes in hot water. We located an old-fashioned wash tub, set up our laundry on the hillside, lit a fire under the tub, and stirred our clothes with a stick. The idea was definitely not as hot as the washing process turned out to be. We were nearly done in.

The laundry, shower, and latrine area was a social gathering place, especially after USAFFE left. I associate the area with one song in particular, "On the Road to Mandalay." Sue and I often sang this with great gusto en route to or from there and while in the showers.

I recall sitting on the hill nearby, watching the sunset over the lake and playing "Home" on the ocarina: "Night covers all and though fortune may forsake me, Sweet dreams will ever take me home. . . ." I was homesick and had wearied of the heat of New Guinea. Because I couldn't go home, I hoped we'd hurry up and get to the Philippines, where there'd be at least some semblance of civilization.

At last, orders came through. The office was closed and we were told to go home and wait to be notified. Once we were packed, a truck took us to the airstrip for a weigh-in. We had to be in full pack, so we boarded the truck wearing helmets, musette bags, pistol belts, canteens, and trench knives. Twenty of us, plus our duffel bags, squeezed into one truck and took off in a drizzling rain.

After we returned from the airstrip, we had to clean our tents in preparation for an inspection. In typical army fashion, someone had forgotten to issue us suntan slacks, so we had to unpack our duffels and stuff in the slacks. We hung around for a day or so before the alert finally came—we were to be ready for departure the next morning at four o'clock.

Some of us stood out on the mountainside that evening and watched the New Guinea sunset for the last time. It was more glorious than ever. Sue, in one of her letters, described it superbly:

New Guinea decided to give us a special send-off that last evening with one of her most extraordinary sunsets. The sky blazed with fiery red-orange that tinged the edges of the clouds and colored the flat surface of the lake a deep blood-red. Gradually, it paled, then darkened into night and one by one the stars appeared, warm and close. Undoubtedly there'd been dozens of other sunsets as lovely, but this one seemed a special performance just for us.

We rode away in darkness the next morning, down the road to the highway and on to a men's mess hall where we had breakfast. From there we went to the airstrip and boarded a C-46 for the Philippines. In a short while, New Guinea was only a memory.

Eight

Heading north, we quickly passed over the equator (Hollandia is only two degrees south of it). We proceeded toward Peleliu, in the Palau Islands, a halfway stopover on our way to Leyte, in the Philippines. Peleliu was a coral island of pure white sand, so dazzling in the sunlight that looking at it hurt our eyes. As a prelude to the Leyte invasion and the ultimate retaking of the Philippines, the navy felt that wresting Peleliu from the Japanese was strategically important.

The island was largely ridges honeycombed with caves that had been converted into fortresses, thus enabling the enemy to mount fierce resistance to the invading 1st Marines and the Army 81st Infantry Division. Casualties on both sides were horrendous. The United States lost more than 1,000 killed and 5,000 wounded before the island finally fell in September 1944. As it turned out, it was only marginally important in the taking of the Philippines.

Now used as a base, Peleliu had Quonsets, two chapels, and a Red Cross canteen, where we were served doughnuts and coffee. The canteen lounge, the plushest I'd ever seen, had overstuffed blue furniture—marvelous, after not having sat on a soft chair for more than ten months. Not far from the tents of the living area was the cemetery. Hundreds of crosses indicated the sacrifices made to take this tiny island, which can't be found on most current maps. Along the far edge of the cemetery was a thick stand of coconut palms, one of the few signs of plant life on the island.

Having had our snack, we went to take a closer look at the cemetery and read the names on the crosses. No one spoke on our way back to the plane, which had just finished refueling. It was time for takeoff.

The next leg of the journey lasted several hours, during which I saw nothing but the ocean below. Once, we ran into a severe squall and had to fly on instruments, but it was smooth after that. One of the pilots let me take over. From then on, whenever I saw a C-46, I proudly said to myself, "I flew one of those."

Tacloban, Leyte, Philippine Islands
June 17–18, 1945

The Japanese decided that we would launch a major campaign to recover the Philippines at Leyte and its adjoining gulf. Leyte would readily accommodate an armada necessary for landing troops and all the necessary equipment and supplies required for an invasion. From the patterns of our advance across the South Pacific, they concluded that we would strike at Leyte before taking on the already heavily defended Luzon.

They fortified the island and brought in thousands of men, eventually more than 50,000. The Americans deployed seven divisions, which participated in the heavy fighting around the capital, Tacloban. One of the divisions was Jim's 1st Cavalry. American as well as Japanese casualties were staggering. So were those of the navy in the Leyte Gulf, the greatest battle in their history. Except for mopping up after the fighting, the Leyte campaign had lasted about two months.

Late in the afternoon, under cloudy skies, we landed on the airstrip at Tacloban. Waiting trucks took us along a level dirt road toward the camp where we were to spend the night before going on to Manila. The dust rose in great billows, adding to the weight of the already limp vegetation along the roadside. What we didn't leave in a cloud behind us settled on our clothes and in our hair. We soon reached the Women's Casual Camp, which was used for transient USO personnel, nurses, Red Cross workers, and Wacs, most of whom were en route to other bases, particularly on Luzon.

While we were settling in, a downpour began. It was now dark, and we'd had nothing to eat since five o'clock that morning except doughnuts and coffee at Peleliu. We lost no time in getting to the mess hall when supper was announced. Alas, what awaited us was sauerkraut, tepid, dehydrated mashed potatoes, stale bread, jungle butter, and coffee best described as boiled mud. We ate it anyway, then waded through water that came halfway to our knees and spent a miserable night crowded ten to a tent.

During the night the water drained off, leaving a morass of dank, smelly mud. The road we'd ridden the evening before was now wet and slippery, but the vegetation, washed by the rain, looked fresh and green. We breakfasted on doughnuts and coffee at the airstrip, then took off in the faithful C-46 for Luzon.

It was comfortably cool in the plane—the first time I'd been cool since I left Colorado the year before. Margie Morris tried to play the air corps song on her slide whistle. Then the pilot passed back word that we'd be over Manila in fifteen minutes, and he dropped down to 2,000 feet so we could have a good look at the city. It was in ruins. Among scattered areas of rubble, streets were discernible, winding around the debris of the war. Houses and high-rise buildings were now shells—roofless, contiguous walls of almost white stone. It looked like a gigantic archaeological site in the process of being excavated.

After passing northward over numerous villages scattered among rice paddies and cultivated cane fields, we approached Clark Field. Clark Field and Manila were the major objectives in the Allied advance toward Japan, and the area around the airfield was the scene of a bitter battle. Debris and tangled wrecks of planes, many our own, had been pushed aside to clear the runways. We touched down at last and found Lieutenant Thomas with an air corps captain waiting for us.

Luzon, Philippine Islands
June 18–November 1, 1945

The captain insisted on our coming to his area for lunch before we started the trip by truck for our new camp at San Miguel. We walked to another runway a short distance away where his C-47 was waiting to transport us. We climbed aboard the plane, which had cots instead of seats. The trip was only an eight-minute hop. When we landed, the group split, half of us going to the officers' quarters and the other half going to the EM area. I chose to go with the former.

The captain's outfit was located on an old Spanish plantation that, before the war, was probably the wealthiest in that part of Luzon. Characteristically, it had been run like a feudal system, with the landowner living in a grand house and the local peasants, little more than serfs, provided with barely enough to subsist.

The officers were quartered in an old, once-elegant two-story wooden house, slightly in need of paint and repair but nonetheless charming in its tree-shaded setting. Along one side of the house was a large tiled patio with a tall tree growing in the center. The gardens surrounding the patio contained a variety of plants, trees, and flowering shrubs, the loveliest of which was a magnificent flame tree.

The captain gave us a tour of the house, proudly showing us the bar, lounge, bathroom, and living quarters. Everywhere there were Spanish-style tiled floors with floral designs in blues and greens. After having a drink at the bar, which was the officers' special pride, we were served lunch on the patio by Filipino boys. What a contrast to the wilds of New Guinea.

After lunch, there was still time to look around the grounds before returning to Clark Field. I followed a path through the gardens that led to an octagonal private chapel with an altar and a large crucifix in the center. Behind the altar was the family burial plot, once tiled over but badly desecrated by the Japanese in their search for gold and other jewelry. A nearby mausoleum was similarly ravaged. Metal doors of the individual burial vaults were ripped off or hung loosely, exposing skulls and bones of the plantation's former owners. Although these people had lived luxuriously by exploiting the local population, I resented the barbarism of the invaders.

It was time to go. We walked to the little airstrip, boarded the C-47, and in minutes were back at Clark Field, where a truck was waiting to take us to our new camp at San Miguel in Tarlac Province, some twenty-five miles north.

Except for our view from the air, we hadn't seen the Luzon countryside until we began our truck trip to San Miguel from Clark Field. The route we followed was the one taken by our armies as they drove south from Lingayen Gulf to Manila. Evidence of the war was everywhere. Shells of houses were patched with bamboo, tin, and thatch to make them habitable. Many more were demolished except for a flight of stone steps leading to empty space or scattered rubble. Wrecked planes rusted in the tall grass beyond the rice paddies and patches of sugarcane. The war itself had gone elsewhere, leaving the land once more serene and the people going about their traditional ways.

We passed groups of Filipinos along the road. The women and older girls looked neat and clean in their light cotton dresses, conical *buri* hats, and wooden sandals, but many of the small children looked scruffy and disheveled. Although all the little girls wore dresses, many of the boys were nude below their waist-length, drab-colored T-shirts. The children waved to us or made the V-for-victory sign, calling "Vic-tor-ee Joe!" Others stared; we were the first women GIs they'd ever seen.

The carabao were numerous. They pulled homemade carts with solid wooden wheels, or were driven along the roadside by small boys who apparently were their caretakers. The slow-moving animals plodded along the dusty roadside or wallowed in large pools of viscous mud that had collected from the overflow of rice paddies. Some carabao were completely submerged except for their eyes, ears, and nostrils. The heat and humidity were relentless, but absorbed in my latest adventures, I no longer minded.

San Miguel was a hamlet consisting of a number of thatched huts, a restaurant, and a gas station. We turned off the highway and drove about three miles along a dusty dirt road to Camp San Miguel.

San Miguel, Tarlac, Philippine Islands
June 18–October 22, 1945

The camp was on a slight rise in the middle of a flat valley floor so wide that the enclosing mountains, with the exception of Mount Arayat, were barely discernible. Much like the plantation near Clark Field, the heart of San Miguel consisted of three fine, old two-story houses that stood in a large grove of tall trees. The headquarters of the camp, which was a signal corps and Australian wireless installation, was in the grandest of the homes. The second home, which was less pretentious, had served as quarters for Japanese officers and had suffered considerable misuse. The WAC detachment orderly room occupied the third home, an ordinary building that had been used perhaps for housing servants. A flight of outside steps led to a small screened porch that served as an entrance to the orderly room and the CO's office.

Unlike the men, who lived in squad tents, the 120 Wacs who constituted the detachment lived in barracks, which the army built in unshaded areas near the tall trees that surrounded the main buildings of the camp. The barracks, accessed by a small flight of steps, had corrugated tin roofs and were half-enclosed with tar paper attached to the framework. Spaces about two feet above the wooden floor and six to eight inches below the siding were left for ventilation. Later, when the tar paper proved inadequate for the rainstorms that hit the area, army engineers covered the siding with corrugated tin. The result, in the terrible heat of July, was comparable to a blast furnace.

The chapel, under construction by Filipino carpenters when we arrived, consisted of a twin-gabled tent with sides of woven bamboo called *sawali*. Inside, planks supported by upright wire spools served as sturdy but uncomfortable benches for the congregation. Both chaplin and choir had to compete with the din of dump trucks rumbling along the road nearby and the droning of northward bound B-24 bombers from Clark Field. Despite these drawbacks, services were well attended.

The completed chapel was an attractive and thatch building with a vestibule, a twin-gabled roof and two towers, the taller of which supported a large, but simple bamboo cross. Shortly after the chapel was finished, Sue persuaded me to sing in the choir.

We were restricted to camp on our first eight to ten days at San Miguel because of enemy activity. Our military was conducting sweeps to capture remnants of the Japanese army who had become separated from their forces and were hiding in the vast field of *kunai* grass along the edge of the camp. The Japanese were trying to link up with one another and work their way north, where heavy fighting was still in progress. At night they signaled one another with red flares that flashed like Fourth of July fireworks, and we'd hear the rapid fire of what we supposed were the light machine guns of our patrols. Our men caught twenty-five of the stragglers during that period, one of whom had broken into our mess hall to steal some food. We weren't worried. All they wanted was food, not us.

We went to work right away in the smaller hacienda where various rooms became our offices. As in the other homes of Spanish landowners, the floors were beautiful and the woodwork and tiles of fine quality. However, the Japanese had ruined the plumbing. When it ceased working, they ripped it out and threw it in a corner. There was a pile of toilet parts, broken tiles, and bits of plumbing pipe in the pantry off the kitchen where Bell, Gremmy, and I worked. The walls were bare except for lizards that moved occasionally or made funny noises that may have been mating calls. Behind me was the shell of a refrigerator from which the Japanese had torn out the motor and shelving, wrecking the door hinges in the process. From the windows beside me I could smell the sweet aroma of gardenias that grew along the side of the house. The scent of gardenias still reminds me of this hacienda.

We continued working on the same shipping code for a short while. Then, one of the many Filipino women who did laundry for people in the camp returned a bundle that was wrapped in pages from a Japanese air codebook. A feverish search was on to locate the woman and all the customers to whom she'd delivered laundry.

The discovery was fortuitous. At that time, the Japanese air force could no longer operate effectively in the Philippine area, but it was having considerable success in the China theater. Our military was eager to get all the information it could from the air codes in order to curtail the heavy losses we were incurring there. By tracking down the laundresses, signal corps personnel managed to recover a significant number of pages of the codebook, so we spent the remaining weeks of the war working on this air code.

Living conditions at our new camp, except for the heat and insects, were a vast improvement over those in New Guinea. We had a greater variety of food, which included fresh eggs, fried chicken, canned beans, spaghetti, and lots of rice. There was a GI saying, "Jesus Christ, no more rice and no more beans in the Philippines."

Instead of going to parties or picnicking to supplement our boring fare, as we had in New Guinea, we could go to Filipino restaurants and get fried chicken whenever we wished. Our cooks served lots of spaghetti, which caused considerable griping. We had it for our first lunch the day after we arrived. The heat was insufferable, and I was in no mood for hot, starchy food, especially something with tomatoes in it. I left the mess hall and stood in line waiting to dump it into the garbage before washing my mess kit in the can of soapy water. As I approached the garbage can, I saw several small, raggedy children holding varied containers to collect the garbage we were throwing away. One little girl who had been pushed aside by the larger children had no container and was holding out her hands to get my garbage. Her big round eyes were imploring. As I watched the spaghetti I'd just been griping about slither into her tiny outstretched hands, I was so overcome with remorse and compassion that I nearly broke down and cried on the spot. I have never forgotten those little hands.

All water in the camp had to be brought in, so its use was limited to drinking, showers, and washing clothes. We were allowed one shower a day and enough water for drinking and washing small items. We gave our shirts and pants to Filipino laundry women, who came to the camp daily. They waited around, sitting on their heels, smoking (some put the lighted ends in their mouths), and talking to one another, hoping for business. It was standard practice for us to settle on a price and provide the soap, and the laundresses would return the clothes starched and ironed. As mud puddles where ubiquitous, many of the women used the water for washing the clothes, which they then hung in trees or on fences to dry. When it rained, it was necessary to dry the clothes over fires, which usually produced a horrid, pungent smoke that permeated the clothes and persisted after they'd been starched and ironed.

I tried several of the women but they proved unsatisfactory. Sometimes items were missing, but the chief problem was the smoky odor of the clothes. Then I found Corazon Romero, who did sewing as well as laundry. She had saved her sewing machine by burying it before the Japanese reached the area, no mean accomplishment considering the heavy tropical rains that deluged the island during the four years it lay buried.

Corazon and I became friends, and after her second child was born she asked me to be its godmother. I was flattered and honored. Unfortunately, I had to miss the christening because I was transferred to Manila for return to the States.

Although camp life at San Miguel was an improvement over that in New Guinea, we still had to contend with intense heat. Merely sitting still could generate sweat. In late July the heat had become so oppressive by midafternoon that we changed our schedule and began work at 6:00 A.M. One noon as I came out of the mess hall I had to sit down and hang my head between my knees to keep from fainting. All of us had lost weight. I melted off ten pounds, which I could hardly spare. Some, like Cady, developed rashes and were extremely uncomfortable. Fortunately, the heat diminished rapidly by nightfall, and though evenings weren't as cool as those on our mountainside in New Guinea, they were fairly pleasant.

When we weren't struggling with the climate or waging war against the Japanese by pushing pencils in our offices, we were doing battle with ants and cockroaches in the barracks. Most effective against the ants were our antproof shelves, suspended from the timber by shoestrings dipped in GI insect repellent. The cockroaches were another matter. These nocturnal pests were a small winged variety that flew around erratically, smacking against us or hitting the walls with a splat. Sue procured a Freon bomb and blasted them while I stomped on any that tried to escape. A little breathless, we counted our bag—Sue got 164 and I killed 30 with my size nine Li'l Abners.

Despite the rigors of climate and the inroads of ants and roaches, we were eager to explore the fascinating country that surrounded us. Manila was first on the list. As soon as the camp restriction was lifted, Sue and I, among others, got overnight passes, swung aboard the "Manila Express" (a two-and-a-half-ton army truck), and headed for the big city.

We rolled along the wide, flat countryside with its rice paddies and cane fields. Water buffalo stood in the flooded paddies, a sleeping boy spread-eagle across the back of his muddy charge. Scattered among the paddies and fields were ruins of small haciendas, little remaining except chimneys rising above the rubble. In the shimmering distance emerged the faint outline of a low volcano.

As we approached the city, the scene changed—paddies and fields yielded gradually to small truck farms, and the road became congested with pedestrians, assorted army vehicles, and *cartellas,* which were the two-wheeled, pony-drawn, roofed carts that served as the principal means of civilian transportation.

As we entered the city we saw a large traffic circle in the center of which was a tall, two-tiered stone monument on a stepped platform. Beside it, a sign warned GIs about the dangers of drinking bad whiskey, and for emphasis listed the number of deaths and blindness currently caused by it. The road divided and we drove along Rizal Avenue, one of two main boulevards leading into central Manila. Dr. José Rizal was a gifted intellectual martyred by the Spanish for his revolutionary writings. On our left was the Chinese cemetery with its stately marble mausoleums and cenotaphs, which were largely intact despite the surrounding destruction. This part of the city had been a residential area graced with beautiful homes, now reduced to piles of rubble, twisted iron rods, and crumbling, shell-mutilated roofs.

We crossed the recently restored Quezon Bridge over the Pasig River and came into central Manila. On either side of us were shapeless heaps of concrete and distorted girders that emerged from the skeletons of what had once been grand hotels, department stores, banks, and public buildings—sad reminders of a city that had been noted for its charm and beauty. Every block or so, the street wound around accumulations of stone and debris that lay where they had fallen after the bombardment. Tucked among the ruins were tiny open-air restaurants, souvenir shops, photo galleries, and numerous honky-tonks, all hastily assembled from corrugated tin, boards, shipping crates, or whatever materials were readily available.

Soon we became engulfed in traffic. Beleaguered MPs strove desperately to sort out the chaos of military vehicles, *cartellas*, working crews with their equipment, and pedestrians, all eager to get to their respective destinations.

Manila was booming. Its population was supported mainly by the military; in turn, the civilians provided them with goods and entertainment. Shops offered a wide variety of hand-produced goods: hats, mats, and handbags of woven rattan, wooden sandals in garish colors, objects of carved carabao horn, and decorative wooden boxes. Honky-tonks served "rotgut" rum and whiskey, strident amateur bands provided music for dancing, and in the darker recesses of the city, other forms of pleasure were easily obtainable.

Motley crowds swarmed the streets: military of every rank and service; pastel-clad Filipino men; women in print dresses, many with babies on their hips; ragged children; merchants and vendors with their varied-colored wares. It was a veritable potpourri of humanity. Our eyes, accustomed to the uniformity of military "suntans," were distracted by the spectrum of color that confronted us. After our life in remote New Guinea and our cloistered two weeks in Camp San Miguel, the entire scene was both fascinating and bewildering.

The crowd ahead of us parted to make way for a contingent of Australian POWs who were coming down the street.

What a heartrending sight these frail, emaciated men were as they shuffled wearily along, their cavernous eyes in expressionless faces, looking straight ahead, oblivious of the staring, silent crowd. Who could have guessed they were homeward bound? The city through which they walked those last dusty miles on their journey home could be repaired, but the scars of these miserable men might never be healed. I pushed the troubling thoughts to the back of my mind as we moved along with the crowd.

We forgot to eat, not enticed by the tiny open-air restaurants with their unvaried menus of greasy fried chicken and rice, served at tables with grimy tablecloths and wilting flowers stuck in tin cans. We decided to go to the Red Cross club.

The club occupied a three-story building with a canteen on the first floor, a recreation room on the second, and a top floor that was probably offices. The canteen was crowded with hungry GIs who had formed several chow lines to receive free coffee, sandwiches, and doughnuts. The recreation room, covering the entire second floor, contained tables where one could play table tennis, shoot pool, or play cards. We decided to forgo indoor recreation in favor of eating and shopping. I bought table mats for friends, two carved, wooden boxes for my sisters, and a letter opener of carabao horn for myself.

Coming out of the Red Cross club, we saw a drunken sailor who kept trying to pull a post out of its concrete moorings. He tugged away, cursing, then sighed and slowly collapsed. Silence. Soon he stirred, pulled himself up, and renewed his efforts. A small crowd gathered, egging him on. The entertainment was cut short when a whistle blew and two shore police (SPs), pushing their way through the onlookers, carted him off to a nearby truck containing others in various stages of intoxication. Collecting sailors who had overindulged and taking them back to their ships was one of the regular duties of the SPs in Manila.

Someone recommended that we see Chinatown, so we walked over to look around. We saw a Chinese man whose every visible tooth was capped with gold. I wondered how he managed to escape being "done in" for his unusual bank account. That section of the city looked menacing. After a short while we left; we had to return to the WAC detachment before Manila's 11:00 P.M. curfew.

My second trip to Manila far surpassed the first. Bob Mason, a classmate of mine at Fredonia, discovered that I was at San Miguel and came to see me. Bob was a good-looking but very shy basketball star. Numerous girls had crushes on him, but I knew of no one he'd ever dated. I couldn't help but think, Oh, boy, if they could only see me now. He was lean, tanned, and handsome in his lieutenant's uniform, and he invited me to go to Manila the next day—in a jeep.

We spent most of the afternoon exploring the part of Manila known as Intramuros, or the walled city. The Spaniard Legaspi erected a fortress there on the edge of the Pasig River in 1571 after his victory over the Muslims. Later, it was attacked unsuccessfully by the Chinese, after which the Filipinos built a wall around the fortress and the settlement that had grown up beside it. Over the centuries the walled fortress successfully withstood attacks by the Dutch, Portuguese, and Sulu pirates, only to meet total destruction by the occupying Japanese and the air and ground forces of the United States.

The Japanese had burrowed into every nook and cranny of Intramuros, making it virtually impossible to flush them out without completely ravaging the historic city. It was a mass of concrete debris. Already, vegetation had begun to take root and was creeping into cracks and crevices of the rubble. We walked around looking at sections of walls and houses that were still standing, then went to St. Augustin Church. Except for sections of the roof of the nave, it was pretty much intact. The priest, wearing a soiled long white garment and heavy GI shoes without socks, met us at the entrance and conducted us around. He showed us where the Japanese had set up a machine gun on the altar and mowed down the Filipinos as they scurried for shelter from the fighting. Rain had come through holes in the roof and left puddles on the floor. Here and there were shreds of clothing and a few moldy shoes left after the bodies had been taken out. We followed the priest up a flight of stairs to the choir loft. There, sections of chairs and benches, bits of fallen roof, and pieces of choir music lay about. I would like to have taken a sheet of the music, which was on parchment with rectangular notes and looked very old. We thanked the priest, gave him some money for reconstruction, and left.

That evening Bob took me to dinner at a lovely restaurant. After seeing nothing but "greasy spoons" on my first trip, I was pleasantly surprised to learn that Manila had decent places to eat. Afterward, we went to a nightclub and danced on the roof, where there was an extraordinary view of the city.

We went back to Manila a second time and had dinner at the China Grill, a cocktail lounge and restaurant on Rizal Avenue in the downtown part of the city. Afterward, we drove along Rizal Avenue to the Chinese cemetery. Many of the tombs were built like actual houses or pagodas, and Bob told me that some had been equipped with toilets and refrigerators as well as other household furniture. All were used for both the living and the deceased.

It was a bright moonlit night. We drove around parts of the city that were virtually deserted, looking at the ruins. To get the full effect of the eerie scene, Bob turned off the headlights and drove by the light of the moon. I felt that whatever I might see of Manila after that would be an anticlimax. He dropped me off at La Salle College, where enlisted women were required to stay when visiting the city. We returned to San Miguel the next day. Bob was transferred the following week and I never saw him again.

Nine

The chief town in Tarlac Province was Tarlac, the provincial capital, eight miles from our camp at San Miguel. Before units of the U.S. Sixth Army, with some 68,000 troops, had driven through the area, engaging the Japanese along the way, Tarlac had been a town of 35,000 people. There had been stores, public buildings, lovely homes, and numerous churches, mostly dominated by the Spanish who owned the sugar plantations. Now the town was gutted, the main street a row of open-front shops, tiny restaurants, and "nightclubs" selling gin and rum made at a local distillery and featuring the music of blaring Filipino bands.

Whenever we went into town, we were followed by a retinue of small, raggedy children. Once Bell and I counted twenty who were trailing closely behind us. In the little restaurants, we sat at tables and chairs like those found in stateside ice cream parlors of the 1920s. When we were served, the owner and/or his wife would pull up a chair to watch while we ate, and a little group of observers gathered outside. At first I thought being Wacs was the reason for such diligent attention, which continued until the day we left, but male GIs were watched with equal curiosity. (A cartoon in

Yank magazine showed Sad Sack with a retinue gaping at him while he took a shower and sat on the latrine.)

One evening I tried the bowling alley. The pins were "duck" pins and the bowling balls were the size of softballs. It was not a game of skill. The alleys were miniature roller coasters, and the sport consisted of guessing the direction the ball was going to take after descending a hump in the alley. The pin boys jumped aside delightedly when a hit was scored.

One day Bell and I went out of the camp to hitch a ride to Tarlac. A Filipino GI, slim and neat in a freshly starched uniform, stood by the roadside while we waited for someone to come along. A weapons carrier, driven by a sergeant, stopped to pick us up. Bell and I hopped in front, and just as the Filipino started to climb in, the sergeant let out the clutch with a jerk and took off, leaving the GI standing in the road. We got a glimpse of his embarrassed, smiling face as the dust settled down over him. Bell and I were seething and demanded to be let out, whereupon the sergeant called us "goddamn gook-lovers" and worse epithets, insulting us personally and denigrating the Corps. The little Filipino may have been one of the many guerrillas who had been risking his life during the Japanese occupation while the bigoted driver was living in the safety and relative comfort of Brisbane.

To me, Tarlac couldn't compare to the cozy familiarity and charm of the small barrio of Mapalasaio, a couple of miles away from the camp. It was frequented mostly by Aussies of a radio intelligence unit attached to CB. The hangout was Mrs. Guinto's, a ground-level house that served as her home and a cafe. "Tex" Ruthven introduced me to "the barrio" and Mrs. Guinto's. Tex was a happy-go-lucky redhead with a splendid physique who had been a Golden Gloves contender. Unlike my idea of a boxer, he was witty and intelligent and appeared to come from a good family. He was well known to the Filipinos, of whom he was fond, so Mrs. Guinto always managed to give us a table even if the cafe was crowded.

The cafe consisted of two rooms attached to the living quarters, separated by a woven bamboo-thatch wall. These rooms were dimly lit by oil lamps and contained eight to ten tables and "ice cream parlor" chairs. Mrs. Guinto's specialty was fried chicken with *camotes*, a sweet root vegetable cut like thick potato chips and deep-fried in what I presumed to be carabao oil. The feast might be temporarily interrupted by having to lift our feet as an occasional pig or chicken meandered through, looking for tidbits that might have fallen on the earth floor. Music was provided by Mrs. Guinto's teenage nephew, who played the guitar and sang sad, romantic songs in English and Spanish. He developed a crush on me, and each time I went there he sang a song that had drawn a response from me, the first time he played it:

> *Whistling in the dark,*
> *I see the lights all over town*
> *While I am walking up and down*
> *without a single thing to do. . . .*

He would look at me with soulful eyes as he sang. I was always touched.

Other musical entertainment was more raucous. The Aussies in the other room, who brought along some of their own beer and a concertina player, obliged us with frequent renditions of "Waltzing Matilda" and " 'Aome, 'Aome on the Rynge." What could compare to Mrs. G's?

One night Tex and I had to hitch a ride back with some GIs who had a weapons carrier. One of the fellows, who was called "Loudermilk," was so drunk that he had difficulty getting aboard. As soon as we took off, he was determined to climb out of the truck. After a couple of attempts, a concerned GI said, "Somebody's going to have to hit the son-of-a-bitch." Somebody did, Loudermilk went down, and that was the end of that.

Once, Tex and I were invited to dinner with some of his Filipino friends. They lived in a little house on stilts, like most of those in the barrio. The grandmother, who was sitting on the ladderlike steps smoking a cigar butt when we arrived, came down to let us pass. She was barefooted. We climbed up and were ushered into a main room about twelve to fifteen feet square with two windows and a floor made of split bamboo.

Because there was no furniture, we sat cross-legged on the floor. No one sat down to eat with us. The hostess brought in trays of rice, fried chicken, and sliced mango, then stood back against the wall to watch us. As we ate I could look down through the strips of the bamboo floor at the family's pigs and chickens below.

I thought we'd finished when she took our trays, but to my surprise she returned with the *pièce de résistance,* ice cream. Following her were about ten people, mostly adults and older children, who had come to watch us enjoy the treat. They filled the room. The ice cream, served in ordinary drinking glasses, had melted to a flaky mass about the size of a walnut floating in a milky-colored fluid. It was frozen evaporated milk with rice, sugarcane sweetener, and kernels of American canned corn. We ate it with relish and expressed our delight to the pleased hostess and onlookers. I was deeply moved by the sacrifice these poor people had made to procure the ingredients to make us a delicacy that few of them had ever had. I don't think any other GIs ever visited barrio people in their homes, so to them it was an important occasion.

Another experience that deeply affected me occurred one day when some of us were going into Tarlac. A small crowd had gathered at the edge of town, and the driver stopped so we could find out what was happening. People moved aside to let us look. There lay three dead Japanese. We heard that they had been coming into town with their hands held up in surrender when they were cut down, victims of the people's intense hatred and fear of treachery. The bodies lay naked except for loincloths, looking as peaceful as if they were sleeping. Already, flies were gathering on the little rings of blood around the bullet holes in their torsos. Our driver hurried to the edge of the crowd and vomited. Just then, a big long-bed truck pulled up and two GIs jumped out, took down the tailgate, and went over to the corpses. One lifted the first body by the hands, his partner by the feet, and they swung it onto the back of the truck like a side of beef. It hit the truck bed with a thud. They repeated the procedure with the other two corpses. I seemed rooted to the spot, thinking of the grief of three mothers up in Japan. Why was I thinking of that? The GIs shut the tailgate, climbed in the truck, and drove away.

Gremmy told me the sequel to the story. When she arrived back at San Miguel, someone excitedly said that something was going on in the field outside the camp. She hurried out to see what was happening. A small crowd was watching a bulldozer maneuvering to cover a hole in which the three bodies lay. When a GI rushed over and was trying to extract the gold teeth from one of the corpses, the lieutenant in charge angrily squelched his ghoulish undertaking. The bodies were covered without ceremony.

In our barracks, we were prepared for any enemy that might come our way. Wacs weren't allowed to carry firearms, but there was nothing in the regulations that prohibited our having knives. We had fifteen among us, mostly trench knives, the kind with a thick, sharp, pointed, six by one-and-a-half-inch blade. I had two of these plus a rusting Japanese bayonet. Margie Morris had a jungle machete, a wicked-looking object that she had brought up from New Guinea and kept by her bedside. We slept with the trench knives inside our mosquito nets those first few weeks.

We were put to the test one night as several of us were sitting on our cots talking. Suddenly, the Gremlin's face froze with horror. There, opposite us, was an Asian face looking through the open space between the tin siding and floor of the barracks. Someone managed a shriek, we heard a scuffle, and then the guards were running past. It proved to be a Filipino Peeping Tom, who was immediately caught. Not one of us wielded a knife, bayonet, or machete in our own defense.

There were other Peeping Toms, the aerial variety, who frequently invaded our privacy. Once, a B-24 "buzzing" our area flew so low that we feared for the tin roofs of our barracks, the quarter-million-dollar bomber, and the lives of the foolhardy flyboys. Air force brass must have squelched that bit of derring-do, because it was never repeated.

No one prevented the little Stinson recon planes from buzzing us about fifty to seventy-five feet above the ground. One day, when Jane, Margie, and "Burky" Burkhead were sunbathing, a little L-5 came in low and the occupants waved at them. The girls waved back, whereupon the L-5 circled, came in even lower, and dropped two weighted pieces of paper, which landed at their feet: "Lts. Bird and Gorman would like a couple of dates for Sunday. If it's O.K., wave your hands and we'll land on your strip around 4:00 P.M." Such a novel exploit deserved a reward. They waved.

Lenient air force regulations worked to our advantage when a pilot from Clark Field consented to fly Bell and me to Mindoro to see her brother, an A-20 pilot stationed at San Jose on the southern tip of the island. Our CO, Captain Dillistin, gave us passes and away we went.

When we arrived, we learned to our dismay that Bell's brother was on temporary duty on another island. Some of his friends found accommodations for us at the nurses' quarters and then took us for a jeep ride northward along the shore. We had to leave the next day, because we had only overnight passes. But there was a hitch. An Eighth Army colonel, who apparently had jurisdiction over the air force contingent, wouldn't let us leave without his authorization. He ordered us to report to him.

With trepidation, Bell and I stepped into his office and snapped our smartest salutes. He questioned us heatedly. We were properly meek and "sirred" him at every appropriate opportunity. It was difficult, though, not to bristle when he impugned the intelligence of the officer who had permitted us to come. What was distressing him was the paperwork involved in cutting orders for the return transportation. It looked simple to me:

> The following military personnel are authorized air travel from A.P.O. 321 to A.P.O. 74 (W.A.C. Det. S.I.S.), for the purpose of joining their proper organization:
> T/5 Irene J. Brion A-217606
> Pvt. Harriott Bell A-217743
> BY ORDER OF COLONEL CARUTHERS

We reported to Captain Dillistin upon our return. Her only concern was that Bell had missed seeing her brother.

Two days later, on August 6, the atomic bomb was dropped on Hiroshima. Initially, no one understood its significance. Details weren't forthcoming about the amount of energy released by the bomb. Most of us thought it was just a bigger, more hazardous one. At each subsequent report of its effects, we became increasingly aware of its horrendous potential. Selfishly, we thought primarily in terms of its ending the war rather than its impact on future world politics.

On August 8, immediately after the Russians entered the war, the United States bombed Nagasaki. Many believed that the Japanese could not hold out much longer, but others felt that we would have to use more atom bombs, perhaps even on Tokyo, before they would surrender.

The days that followed were rife with rumors of a forthcoming armistice. The Potsdam Peace Conference had been working on peace plans since July. Then finally, on August 10, the news broke. Emperor Hirohito personally ordered an end to the war.

I was on CQ that night. When the phone rang I expected the usual call of someone wanting to leave a message. It was HQ with the news. Immediately, relief penetrated every pore of my body. I wanted to rush out and tell everyone, but stickler that I was, I remained at my desk. (The GIs would have described my devotion to duty with the scatological term, "chickenshit.")

It had been quiet for a few minutes, then I heard voices shouting and the popping of rifle shots as the news reached the various units around the camp. The noise increased and seemed to come from every direction. Then Bell and Jane burst in, joyously waving cans of foaming beer, to celebrate. I wasn't supposed to have any because I was on duty, but I wasn't going to sit around and watch someone celebrate without me. I joined them. Meanwhile the racket emanating from our mess hall indicated that a hilarious party was in progress. Scroungers had come up with five gallons of GI dispensary alcohol and a sufficient supply of grapefruit juice. Everybody was singing, whooping, and hugging one another in pure joy. My CQ duties ended at midnight when the OR closed, but the party lasted all night.

The Japanese had actually agreed only to a conditional surrender with the provision that the emperor remain as the nominal head of government. Sobering up after the celebrations, we realized that officially we were still at war. Even though most of us had more than enough "points" to be discharged (the army gave points for years of service, time spent overseas, duty in combat zones, and so forth), the army could keep us until negotiations were finally completed. In fact, the settlement could go on forever—perhaps until the Japanese islands had been completely captured and they agreed to our terms. After three days of deliberations while everybody sat tight and waited hopefully, Truman announced on August 14 that the Japanese had agreed to an unconditional surrender. After our exuberant celebrations, and despite the anxious waiting period, the official end of the war seemed like an anticlimax.

That afternoon we saw an unusual sunset. The sun's rays descended through a narrow evanescent cloud, forming a large cross that was illuminated by the pale light of the sky behind it. Was this a repeat of Constantine's vision at the Milvian Bridge, *In hoc signo . . . ?*

The end of the war had little immediate effect on life at San Miguel. The pace of work slackened, but we continued to decipher the same air code. There was always the possibility that some of the messages might yield important information. We continued preparations for moving to Japan, which had actually begun in July in anticipation of an invasion rumored to be scheduled for September.

During those last weeks at San Miguel, I spent much of my free time reading or writing letters. The detachment had acquired a phonograph and records that they played every afternoon. Whoever was playing the records had tastes similar to mine: Spike Jones's "The Great Big Saw Came Nearer," "You Always Hurt the One You Love," and Artie Shaw's "Adios, Mariquita Linda." The latter still evokes feelings of sadness and nostalgia.

Social life was much the same as before, but gradually the fellows we dated moved out and new ones came in from northern Luzon, where they had been fighting just before the war ended. One of these outfits was the 65th Engineers, among whom were some pleasant fellows whom Bell, Sue, Margie, and the Gremlin met at a party. Sue arranged a date for me to go with them to a club in San Fernando. My date was a double for my old movie idol, Errol Flynn. He proved boring, but among the gang of us, it was a fun evening.

The club was a huge, high-roofed building that originally may have been a warehouse. It was filled with dozens of tables except for a space for dancing and a platform for an orchestra. I noticed hamburgers on the menu, so I ordered one and consumed it happily, whereupon Sue said, "Brion, think, have you seen any cows around here?" I hadn't thought, of course, but whatever the meat was, it wasn't tainted, and I didn't get sick. We ordered drinks. Since we were in a nightclub with some pretensions, I didn't stir my drink in the usual GI way, with my forefinger. No spoon had been provided, so I used my knife. When I took it out of the drink, the blade, from which the silver plate was badly eroded, was a mass of tiny bubbles. That "drink" lasted the rest of the evening.

On another occasion, two GIs of the 65th took Bell, Bea Hart, and me on a jeep ride to some of the little towns and villages to the north of San Miguel. We stopped at one place where there were numerous wrecked tanks, both U.S.

and Japanese, scattered around an area of grass and low shrubs. Getting out to explore, Bell, Bea, one of the GIs, and I climbed up on one of the tanks while the other took our picture. Later we learned that a mine had exploded there and killed a similarly curious American soldier.

One day, when I was working, I was told that someone outside wanted to see me. It was Jim. He was on his way south and transport was waiting for him, so we talked only a few minutes—just long enough to arrange a meeting in Manila. He seemed different, but I told myself it was probably due to all he'd been through in the Luzon campaign. I arranged immediately for a pass. Sue, Jane, and the Gremlin came along too; some of the Sig Photo boys were having a party. We went to an apartment that they were using for the occasion and they were waiting for us, all except Jim. He was supposed to have been delayed and was coming along later, but the evening wore on and he never arrived. It was presumed that he'd been included with some of the men in the unit who had been alerted at the last minute and were being sent up to Japan. Besides being terribly disappointed, I was tired, so I stretched out on an old couch and fell asleep. The party went on around me. The next day, when we went back to San Miguel, everyone was a little depressed. A letter of explanation never came.

I met Fred at a 737th Railway Battalion party shortly after the Manila fiasco. We had few common interests, but he was physically attractive and took me to interesting places. Despite the fact that he was somewhat jealous and possessive and had a quick temper that nearly got him into trouble on a couple of occasions, I enjoyed going out with him. He had a jeep, so we went to Paniqui, Rosales, and other places farther afield.

One night I invited him to dinner at the detachment. As

we were about to enter the mess hall, the PA system announced that I had a visitor at the gate. To my amazement, it was Bill Abbay.

The story of Bill goes back to the Depression. He had been hitchhiking and Daddy picked him up and brought him home. Someone had stolen his suitcase when he was riding the rails, so he had no clothing except what he was wearing. All of us liked him immediately. Mom took him in like the son she never had, found clean clothes for him, and tended to his badly blistered feet. He lived with us for nearly a year, working on the farm. Finally Daddy wangled a clerical job for him in East Rochester, no mean accomplishment in 1935. Learning from Bill that his family knew nothing of his whereabouts since he'd left home the previous year, Mom talked him into writing to his mother. Gratefully, she wrote back, and she and Mom carried on a correspondence until Mom's death. From Bill's mother, Mom learned that Bill had been a Phi Beta Kappa at the University of California at Berkeley and had left, against the family's wishes, to travel around the country to get experience for writing a book on the Depression. We learned more one day when he received an official-looking letter from his uncle, Vice Adm. William H. Standley, chief of naval operations, who frequently acted as secretary of the navy for Adm. Claude Swanson when the secretary was ill. Exactly as I expected, Bill had refused to take advantage of his uncle's former prestigious position and was now a private in the 32d Infantry Division.

I took him in to eat with us, after which Fred gracefully bowed out. We spent a wonderful evening catching up on what we'd been doing, reminiscing and sharing our impressions of the war. I didn't see him again—the 32d was moving out—but I received a letter from him shortly afterward.

It was then late August and our new "Barn Club," San Miguel's own enlisted men's nightclub, held its grand opening dance. Fred and I went with Phyllis Pierce and Ronnie Morsch. All of the booths and eighty tables were filled, and a line for the bar extended all the way around the building. Despite the crowd, half of which was standing, we managed some of the dances. They were listed in the program under catchy titles: "The Wac Wiggle," "The Peso Polka," "The Luzon Leap," "The Carabao Cakewalk," "The Rotation Rumba," "The Tarlac Trot," "The Brisbane Bounce."

Two nights later Fred and I went into Tarlac for dinner in the best restaurant in town. It was our last date—the 737th was leaving for Manila for ultimate shipment to the States. I received a postcard from him, but then nothing more. I didn't especially mind; I had just learned that we could sign up for a rest camp at San Esteban on the seashore up in Ilocos Sur Province.

Tent mates, Tex, Gladys, Marge, and Marion on a break outside the quonset.

Gremmy and I and new friends at a mountain village above Lake Sentani.

Our happy homes after USAFFE made off with the canvas roofs.

Chapel and Marine
cemetery, Peleliu, Palau
Islands.

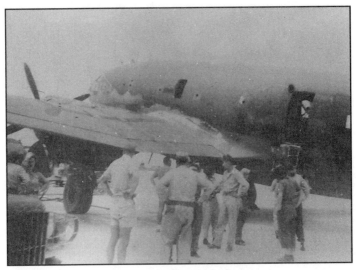

Waiting at Peleliu to take off for the Philippines.

Ravaged beauty of a
Manila public build-
ing. March 1945.

WAC Detachment,
San Miguel, Tarlac
Province, Luzon,
Philippines.

Hacienda at San Miguel where we worked.

Chapel, San Miguel, where Sue and I sang in the choir.

Mail room, San Miguel.

Adjunct of mess hall at San Miguel. Filipinos did most of the cooking.

Entering Manila, looking toward downtown.

At Tarlac, the town nearest San Miguel, where we dined out on chicken and *camotes*.

"Hotshot" Charlie, with whom I shared a narrow escape.

At the Tarlac photographer's "studio," September 1945.

Jane, the SIS. golden girl.

The most moving and inspirational WAC poster.

Marion getting a drink from my pre-war canteen.

The beach at San Esteban on the South China Sea. September 1945.

"Tex" Ruthven, who introduced me to the barrio near San Miguel.

Reading in my tent Sam Esteban. September 1945.

Mike Ryder and I at San
Miguel, before I was transferred to Manila.

WAC Director, Colonel Boyce, her aide, Captain Dillistin, and our lst Sergeant pause during inspection of our camp. September 1945.

Waiting to be shipped home, LaSalle College, Manila. November 1945.

Aboard the Lurline, bound for the States. November 1945.

My decorations: American Campaign Medal, World War II Victory Medal, Philippine Liberation Ribbon, Asiatic Pacific Campaign Medal, Good Conduct Medal, and WAAC Service Medal.

Farewell dinner at the Bismarck Hotel, Chicago. November 28
1945.

Ten

It was an eight-hour drive in a two-and-a-half-ton truck over a terrible road that served as the main highway. We passed through San Fernando and continued north to San Esteban, a sleepy little hamlet on the South China Sea. The SIS camp was situated in a coconut grove, beside a long curve of beach. A tiny lagoon bordered the inland side of the grove, its quiet water reflecting the palms and the thatched houses along its edges. Beyond were the flanking coastal mountains of Ilocos Sur.

In early January 1945, the U.S. Sixth Army landed at Lingayen Gulf and moved southward through central Luzon to clear the area in and around Manila. By the time of my arrival at Camp Esteban, the only obvious reminder of the invasion was a wrecked Japanese barge a mile or so offshore.

Vacationing personnel lived in canvas-roofed structures with raised split-bamboo floors and no siding. A faint sea breeze circulated through the tents, making it comfortable to get out of the sun and read, relax, or take a nap.

There were plenty of ways to relax—swim, sunbathe, walk along the beach and gather shells, explore the native village, or take a raft out to see the multicolored corals of the reef and get a closer look at the wrecked barge. We could also watch the San Esteban fishermen dynamiting for fish, which they brought back to the beach, stretching out the nets to divide the catch. For evening entertainment there were movies and a club for dancing or playing cards and other games.

I spent most of my time looking for shells or reading in my tent. My favorite shell was a hump-backed, cream-colored type with dark brown edges and a dotted brown center. They smelled terrible after I had them a short while, and I spent a good deal of time trying to soak them in soapy water to get rid of the odor—until someone told me to put them in sand where ants could get to them and eat out the insides.

Reading in my tent was fine during the day, except when the PA system blared from late afternoon until midnight— the same old songs, mostly swing—fine for dancing but unbearable for my listening. I wanted to smash the records. Even though I badly needed the change of scene and the leisurely pace at Camp Esteban, I was ready to leave. I felt that getting back to San Miguel might increase my chance of getting home more quickly.

After my return Margie and the Gremlin, both of whom were dating officers (they rarely settled for less), wanted me to meet one of their friends who they thought I would like. He was a riot, they said. He was. Because of his striking resemblance to a character in the comic strip "Terry and the Pirates," he was called "Hotshot Charlie." He was a happy-go-lucky, freckle-faced Irishman from Buffalo, and certainly loads of fun. I dated him several times.

One night we were on our way to Tarlac in his jeep. Nearing a narrow bridge with concrete abutments, we saw a huge truck bearing down on us. The driver obviously had no intention of slowing down, so Hotshot Charlie slowed to let him pass. The truck roared past, crowding us partially off the road. Seeing that we were going to hit the abutment, I jumped from the jeep and rolled into a wide ditch, but Charlie flew into the windshield, cutting his scalp. He wasn't knocked out, but he was too groggy to drive the jeep, which was undamaged except for the cracked windshield. I drove to the nearest dispensary, with Hotshot Charlie making wise-cracks all the way.

The only technician at the dispensary took Charlie into the treatment room, shaved his head around the cut, and asked me to assist him while he put in some stitches. I was fine until he pinched the edges of the cut together and blood oozed out. I came to on the floor with the technician holding a bottle of aromatic spirits of ammonia near my nose. Hotshot Charlie, unattended and still jauntily macho, was chuckling.

Apparently Charlie moved on, because we never dated again.

I met Mike Ryder about that time. I surprised myself by making the first move, which wasn't my style, but when I looked across the Barn Club dance floor and saw a nice-look-ing, suntanned man with light blonde hair in a modified crewcut, I was determined to make his acquaintance. I don't know how I managed it, but I wangled a dance. He proved to be shy, but I could tell he was pleased. After a dance or two, we sat on the sidelines and talked. I felt as if I'd known him a long time, and the same seemed to be true for him. We dated often the rest of the time I was at San Miguel, and he came down to Manila to see me before I left for home.

One night Bell and I decided to attend a party that was advertised on the company bulletin board. About a half dozen GIs arrived in a truck to take us and a number of other

Wacs to the festivities. We had a lot of fun dancing and drinking beer, but it had been a hot day, we were getting tired, and the beer was catching up with us. We decided we'd better be getting home, even if it was early.

Two of the boys who had brought us agreed to take us. Just as we were leaving, four or five of the others who had also brought us said it wasn't fair to leave them out. We were a bit slaphappy, so we told them to come along. When we got to our gate, a cute one said, "Don't I get a good-night kiss?" whereupon the others reminded us of their part in the show. By now, Bell and I were both giddy. We agreed, and they lined up. I went down the line first, with Bell close behind.

Suddenly, I heard a scuffling sound and, turning around, I saw Bell, who was a hefty lady, supporting a GI who had passed out when she kissed him. He hadn't even been tipsy. The guard witnessed the scene and told some of his friends who hung around the camp. Bell didn't dare show her face for a while because she was called "the gal who kisses them cold." Both of us got silent reprimands from a couple of the girls because of our folly.

By early October, SIS was winding down, offices were closing, and personnel were leaving. The rest of us waited for our orders to Manila. During this time, Col. Westray Battle Boyce, the director of the WAC who had replaced Oveta Culp Hobby, was to come to San Miguel to inspect our detachment. She had been on an extensive tour of WAC installations in the Pacific, checking working conditions and morale and probably keeping an eye out for any evidence of exploitation.

We had never heard of Colonel Boyce before. So far as any of us knew, Oveta was still at the helm. An inspection by the director in itself was sufficient to spur us into action, but the name Westray Battle Boyce, added to her exalted position, threw us into a frenzy of preparation.

Colonel Boyce was the antithesis of our expectations. She was young, attractive, and unaffected, and she asked us intelligent and pertinent questions in a friendly, informal way. We were impressed by her graciousness and charm. Before she left we took a picture of her with her aide, Captain Dillistin, and our first sergeant standing outside our barracks door. The inspection was a success. Captain Dillistin received her highest commendation.

When the orders came for us to leave for Manila, during the third week in October, we packed only necessities and traded or gave away everything else to the Filipinos, who came in numbers to the camp. They were eager to get nearly everything we left behind. A top priority was mosquito netting, which they used to make dresses. Never mind the mosquitoes; they were used to them.

La Salle College
Manila, Philippine Islands
October 22–November 3, 1945

Our destination in Manila was La Salle (De La Salle) College, located on Taft Boulevard near the Rizal Memorial Coliseum. At that time, the college, referred to as "Atrocity College" because of the monstrous crimes committed there by the Japanese, housed the overflow Wacs from the main disposition center. It had suffered considerable damage during the battle for the city.

La Salle was a large, rectangular three-story building with two wings perpendicular to the main building. Above the triple-arched entrance was a four-columned portico. The facade was pockmarked from heavy arms fire, and the arched rectangular windows had been replaced with sturdy grill-work. No glass remained. Inside, the foyer showed evidence of considerable fire damage, especially on the ceiling. There had been room-to-room fighting in the classrooms, and an estimated 2,000 people who had taken refuge there were slaughtered. Their bodies had been removed shortly before the arrival of the first Wacs for whom the college was to serve as barracks, but the odor of decay was still so bad that the girls used flowers and perfume on their pillows in order to get to sleep at night.

Machine-gun and shell fire had spattered the rooms, creating holes in the ten-inch walls, tearing off massive chunks of plaster, and exposing the lathes and wooden structure underneath. My room on the first floor, near the lobby, was more severely damaged than most. At the head of my cot was a shell hole about a yard in diameter. I could look through it, get a complete view of the adjoining room, and chat with friends who were bunked there.

The rooms were filled with cots, so close together that there was room only for my duffel bag, which served both as wardrobe and dressing table. The latrine was on the second floor, reached by a flight of damaged marble steps.

La Salle was noisy. Not only were the activities of the Wacs housed there disruptive, but nearby honky-tonks did a thriving business. One had a blaring, inexhaustible orchestra with a limited repertoire. "You Belong to My Heart" was number one of their top ten, and listening to it has always evoked memories of La Salle.

I didn't do much while we waited for the ship. Mike Ryder came down from San Miguel and took me to a USO show in Rizal Stadium. I'd never been interested in going to one—I presumed there'd be a lot of girly dancing geared entirely for men. I was right, but I didn't want to disappoint

Mike after he'd braved seventy miles of a Philippine thoroughfare. Our seats were high in the crowded stadium. A scantily clad dancer was shimmying when one of the men behind me stood up and shouted, "If you wanna play, honey, I'll play with you!" Suddenly a riot erupted. The music increased in volume, but the show went on while the MPs descended upon the rioters. Mike and I, unscathed, rapidly exited.

I had become fond of Mike and dreaded saying good-bye. Ironically, it was I, rather than a boyfriend, who was leaving. I think both of us sensed that this was the end of a special interlude, and that we'd probably never meet again.

One evening when I was assigned to CQ, I was sitting behind the desk in the OR off the lobby. It was hot and sticky and I was edgy. Not looking up, I saw at waist level a khaki figure who had come up to the desk to inquire about someone. I listlessly pushed the visitors' roster toward him. As he bent over the book, I saw his stars. I "shaped up" instinctively, but if he noticed, he made no comment. Here was a general calling on an enlisted woman and not taking me to task for my unmilitary behavior. The war was definitely over.

The long-awaited news came at last. We were to leave Saturday morning, November 3, on the *Lurline*. For the sake of a new experience, I would have preferred a different ship, but the old *Lurline* would make the trip home in fourteen days. It didn't take us long to pack our duffels and get them out in front of La Salle so they could be numbered for efficient loading. Despite thousands of troops boarding ships in Manila Harbor, I never heard of any baggage problems, a lesson airport personnel could learn today.

Eleven

On the trip back to the States, I shared a room with others on B deck, close to the stairs leading up to the promenade deck. It was a considerable improvement over my former "stateroom" on D deck.

On the outbound voyage, the troops had always been on the move, restlessly crawling over each other to get to the opposite side of the ship. Now, everyone sat talking quietly, even dozing, drained of the tensions induced by the war. Days passed. Ship personnel issued us the certificate of the "Domain of the Golden Dragon," recording that we had crossed the international date line on November 12, 1945, at 36° north latitude, 180° longitude. We encountered rough seas shortly afterward and were given tablets to prevent seasickness. The drug had become available since our initial voyage.

As we neared San Francisco, some undercurrent of prescience had spread throughout the ship, and people began hugging the rails to get the first glimpse of home. Finally one night when Bell and I were on the promenade deck, a quickly growing swell of voices arose as people began pushing toward the exits in their rush to get to the port side. We were swept along by the crowd, at the front of it because we had been close to the passageway. At the rail on the other side we saw, on the edge of the horizon, a thin line of faint lights lying like a diamond necklace on the water. Then another parallel line of lights appeared, and another. It looked like a tiara of twinkling points of light. By now the noise of the crowd had faded to a murmur. Many were crying. I was speechless as lines from "America the Beautiful" ran through my head: "Thine alabaster cities gleam, Undimmed by human tears . . ." Our cities were not undimmed by human tears, but in the intensity of my emotion such a thought did not occur to me.

That night we stayed aboard the ship in the harbor. No one slept much. We looked at the lights of the city and chatted about our immediate plans.

Late the next morning we disembarked—more than 2,700 Wacs, 250 army nurses, and a scattering of enlisted men. As I stepped off the gangplank, I wanted to kiss the ground, but there was only the cement dock—hardly an adequate substitute for the soil of my beloved USA. Still, that first step was one of the most stirring moments of my life.

Although newspapers had probably announced the arrival of the *Lurline,* only a few civilians were on the docks. I didn't see any photographers. However, a group of Wacs from Camp Stoneman, professional greeters, or "wavers" as they were called, was there to escort us to a ferry. The fact that only Wacs met us was neither surprising nor disappointing. I would hardly have expected to be welcomed by a crowd of flag-waving, cheering civilians. Unlike the men, we service women weren't regarded as heroines.

The river ferry *Ernie Pyle,* named for a famous reporter killed in the war, was waiting to take us to Pittsburg and from there to the WAC detachment at Camp Stoneman. The ferry was met by the official launch of Camp Stoneman's commandant, which escorted us to the pier. There we were greeted by a band and a small welcoming committee of Wacs.

By the time we'd settled into barracks, all we could think about was our first American meal of fresh, stateside food in fourteen months. We devoured steak, tossed green salad, and a baked potato with sour cream. A dessert of chocolate malted milkshakes topped off our feast. We dragged ourselves back to the barracks, groaning ecstatically. That was the best and the last of our welcome home.

We were at Camp Stoneman for a day or two while we were checked for anything tropically infectious, then we were split up to be shipped to our respective separation centers. Those of us bound eastward boarded a train, alphabetically, for Fort Des Moines, Iowa. Bell, Cady, Marion, and I were assigned to the first car. Everyone else rushed to grab the best seats, passing by the only compartment, which they may have assumed was reserved for an officer or high-ranking noncom. Bell made for the compartment with me in close tow. A harried sergeant stuck her head in and asked what we were doing there, to which Bell confidently replied that we'd been assigned to it. The sergeant hurried on to other business. As the train pulled away, we danced in glee over our coup.

We'd been en route for two to three days when the train slowed and one of the railroad men came through, announcing that we would be stopping for about an hour. We could get off if we wished. For what? We were in the midst of the prairie with no station house in sight.

Then off to our right, about three-quarters of a mile away, we saw the lights of a little town. Suddenly at least 150 Wacs erupted from the train, screeching like banshees and running toward the tiny metropolis. Bell and I managed to be in the spearhead of the attack. We descended upon the sleepy hamlet. It was Thanksgiving Day and everything was closed except a couple of small cafes. Had other trains stopped there? Was that the reason they were open? Stocks were wiped out in minutes, hamburgers were consumed before they'd scarcely been warmed, and people were still outside waiting to get in. Cady didn't bother with a sandwich; she bought a whole turkey and bore it triumphantly back to the train to share with friends. I don't think the town could have survived another unscheduled train stop.

Fort Des Moines, Iowa
November 24–27, 1945

The separation center at Fort Des Moines was organized to discharge personnel as quickly as possible. Upon our arrival, our records were turned in to be checked and prepared while we were undergoing processing. We were divided into groups of twenty-five and provided with a guide who conducted us through all the required phases.

First we took our clothing to the QM to be checked. I was allowed to keep anything I wanted, so I kept my suntans, shirts, dress shoes, trench coat, fatigue dress, and, for sentimental reasons, my helmet, musette bag, mess kit, and one khaki slip. We were issued new winter uniforms and overcoats. The guide took us to our barracks and assigned us cots.

The next step was a physical. I had been worried about this for fear the medics would find something wrong and send me off to a hospital. I needn't have worried. I was healthy and 112 pounds.

Step three was an interview with a counselor to provide her with a summary of our army experience and to receive information regarding veterans' benefits. The last phase consisted of signing the discharge papers and receiving our pay. As we concluded processing, the fort's WAC band, on hand for the occasion, struck up "The WAC Is in Back of You." I felt a tiny sensation of regret, but only for a moment.

During the processing period, we were free in the evening, so Marge, Gladys, Marion, Bell, and I went into Des Moines. We had dinner at a restaurant called Babe's on 6th Avenue, after which we walked around looking for a movie that appealed to us. The best we could do was Walt Disney's *The Three Caballeros*. It was the first civilian movie theater I'd been in since I was in Colorado Springs two years before. The plush seats and interior decoration compensated for the juvenile nature of the film.

The five of us were all ticketed through Chicago, so we decided to stop over on our way home, get ourselves "gussied up," and have a farewell fling. After settling in at the Bismarck Hotel, we headed for a beauty parlor. I had a permanent and a manicure. I'd been nurturing my nails, and they were in perfect condition for my favorite red nail polish. I felt very sleek. That evening we splurged and dined in the Walnut Room of the Bismarck, where a roving photographer took our picture. I made sure that my new manicure was in evidence. Afterward we went to see *The Desert Song,* starring Walter Cassel and Dorothy Sandlin, which was playing at the Studebaker Theatre on Michigan Avenue. The next morning we parted.

The separation was complete. Officially, I was separated from my responsibilities to the U.S. government. I was also separated from a way of life that I treasured in a strange way, even though I never would want to relive it. Personally, I was separated from friends who were really family—family within constant reach, day and night, for seventeen months. For a while, there was still another kind of separation, an inward one, of body from mind. My body went from here to there, but my mind was still there—in a tent in New Guinea, under the big trees by the hacienda in San Miguel, or in the shell-torn skeleton of Manila—a score of places, a score of times. I felt alone in a strange world, a civilian world that I thought I could slip back into so easily.

Glossary

APC The army's cure-all, a pill containing aspirin, phenacetin, and caffeine.

APO Army post office.

ASTP Army specialized training program. College education for all young inductees with high scores on the army's IQ test. Protests that this was undemocratic resulted in disbanding the program and putting the participants into combat infantry divisions with the rank of private.

CB Central Bureau. The Allied international bureau, of which signal intelligence was a branch.

CO Commanding officer.

CQ Charge of quarters. Person in charge of the company office (orderly room) during off-duty hours.

Detail Any assigned job around barracks and immediate areas—for example, kitchen police (KP), CQ, and squad duties such as cleaning latrines and recreation rooms and picking up trash.

Dog tag Metal identification tag listing a soldier's name, rank, serial number, religion, and blood type.

EFS Extended field service. Service outside the continental United States.

GI Government issue. Applies to all articles of clothing and all material things. Also refers to soldiers, replacing the "doughboys" of World War I, and to "prescribed" aspects of behavior. Someone who is GI is very correct and does things by the book. Cigarette butts are GI'd by tearing the paper, scattering the tobacco, and wadding the paper into a tiny ball. GIs also referred to diarrhea—gastrointestinal illness.

Gig A check against you that confined you to the company area and required hourly reporting to the orderly room.

HBT Herringbone twill, a material used in WAC fatigue or combat area slacks.

Li'l Abners WAC field shoes, named for those worn by the cartoon character Li'l Abner.

LRs Latrine rumors. They usually involved something disastrous or undesirable. Most common were those regarding the breaking up of the unit and a transfer to unpleasant places. The most frequent LR at Camp Carson was that we were all going to be sent to Mitchell Field on Long Island (New York was not a popular place). Another sent us to Camp Hale in Leadville, Colorado, where, at 10,000 feet elevation, it was cold most of the year.

MPs Military police, usually army.

NCOs Noncommissioned officer (or noncom) ranking from corporal to first sergeant.

Nisei One born in America of Japanese immigrant parents.

OCS Officer Candidate School.

OD Olive drab. The color of winter uniforms. Also the color of the flat paint on army vehicles, buildings, and equipment.

OR Orderly room. The company office, the domain of the first sergeant. Next to this was the CO's office. In the same building would be an extra room or two, one of which was the supply room.

POE Point of embarkation.

QM Quartermaster. A large central warehouse that housed the supplies for the base.

Sawali Tagalog term for a coarse, woven article of layered bamboo stripsused for baskets, partitions, and sides of houses.

Seabees Members of U.S. Navy construction battalions that built naval aviation bases and facilities.

Section 8 Section of army regulations that grants a discharge to the mentally unstable.

SP Shore police, the naval equivalent of an army MP.

Tokyo Rose American woman in Tokyo who broadcast propaganda aimed at undermining the morale of Allied troops.

USAFFE U.S. Armed Forces in the Far East. All WACs, except AirWACs, were attached to either USAFFE or USASOS (U.S. Army Services of Supply), both under the operational control of general headquarters.

V-mail One-sheet letter that was reproduced photographically, reduced to conserve space, folded to form an envelope, and sent by air rather than surface.

WAAC Women's Army Auxiliary Corps.

WAC Women's Army Corps.

WAVES Women Accepted for Volunteer Emergency Service (navy).

The SIS Family

Tsgt. Ruth "Tex" Hamilton, from Waco, Texas, had been a Spanish teacher in Waco High School prior to the war. She had a marvelous sense of humor, a pithy wit, and was self-assured and confident. Everyone had a healthy respect for her. If there was a problem for us as a group, Tex interceded with the brass, speaking her mind freely but tactfully, and wrongs were quickly righted. When she was younger, she and her sister were attending a bullfight in Spain where they had box seats among the wealthy patrons. A messenger appeared, bearing a note for Tex. It was an invitation for a private dinner with Generalissimo Franco. He waved to her from a nearby box, from which he had apparently been admiring her, for she was a very attractive brunette. Tex refused, but she regarded the incident as her "claim to infamy." She was forty-two and, except for Bea Hart, much older than the rest of us.

Ssgt. Elizabeth McBeath was a "sleeper." Not one to throw a word away, it was a while before we learned that she had a keen, incisive mind and a dry sense of humor. From Plaquemine, Lousiana, she had the quiet, unhurried, soft-spoken manner often associated with southerners. She was the quintessential lady, but a lady with a twinkle.

Cpl. Mary "Ginny" Blakemore, from Emory, Virginia, was graduated from the Agnes Scott School before enlisting in the WAC. She was tall and slim, with fine features and a pleasant, amiable expression. Ginny was serious about her Christianity and involved herself in a variety of jobs for the chaplain, one of which was playing the field organ for Sunday services and other occasions—a task she performed with enthusiasm and considerable skill. She also devoted a lot of time to the boys in the hospital, a humane and appreciated service. Ginny was fun-loving and warmhearted, a definite asset to our group.

Cpl. Mary Summerhalter, the "Gremlin" or "Gremmy," was always annoyed when asked where she was from, usually the most frequently asked question when people met each other in the army. The reason, I suppose, was that she had no permanent home after the death of her mother. Officially, she was from Olney Springs, Colorado. Gremlin was a twenty-three-year-old brunette, petite, and talented artistically. She was also pretty in a birdlike way. Sometimes at work she'd pass me a funny cartoon or a poem. She was adventuresome and was good at coming up with mischievous ideas.

T5g. Marjory "Margie" Morris, from Benton, Pennsylvania, was a petite brunette. Her favorite pastime was sneaking out with officers, chiefly for the thrill of the risk involved. The higher the rank, the better; second lieutenants stood little chance. When the war was over and dating officers was permitted, much spice went out of her life—until passage of the rule that enlisted Wacs weren't allowed in officers' clubs. The challenge gave Margie a new grip on life. Sometimes she and the Gremlin would both be in on these misadventures, and they'd give Bell and me full reports of the subterfuges taken by all parties involved in the execution of the "mission." Margie's accounts were sprinkled with rural Pennsylvania colloquialisms and accentuated by infectious tee-hees.

Pfc. Sue Cross, who had been a laboratory technician in the Philadelphia area, was the dominating figure in the group. She was extroverted, self-assured, talkative, compassionate, intelligent, an intent listener, dynamic, and aggressive. Sue knew where to go when she wanted something—to the top—and she lost no time in getting there. She was never ruthless or overly ambitious, and for the most part didn't hurt or offend people. I liked and admired her immensely.

Pfc. Mary Jane Ford was a tall, striking blonde from a wealthy Carmel Valley, California, family. Seemingly brusque and aloof, she was really shy and self-conscious. Jane was also argumentative and had frequent altercations with Sue, who was her closest friend. Except for one tiff when they didn't speak to each other for a few days, their disagreements were full of sound, devoid of fury, and signified little. In fact they added spice to the daily routine. Jane's effect on men was electrifying, but she remained cool, accepting without acknowledging the attentions of most, but not all of them. She was an excellent swimmer and diver, stopping all activity at our swimming pool in Hollandia when she arrived and strode out on the diving board. It was her skill and strength, as well as her courage, that saved her from drowning and won her the Soldier's Medal. Sue nicknamed her "Fearless," but the rest of us just called her Jane.

Pfc. Helen "Genks" Genkins, an ex-teacher from Brighton, Iowa, was an easy-going, all-around person with a whimsical sense of humor. Genks was quiet and rarely participated in our animated discussions that so frequently ended in arguments, yet she would be there, sitting back and enjoying the action.

Pfc. Juanita "Nita" Howell had been a teacher in Mobile, Alabama, before enlisting. When I first met her at Vint Hill,

I was bored by her seeming inanities. Had I known we were going to be tent mates someday, I'd have cracked on the spot. As it turned out, Juanita proved to be a cheerful, generous, and thoughtful person whom I genuinely liked. During her day off, she cleaned and tidied up the tent, made unmade cots, and had everything in order when we arrived home hot, dusty, and tired. Once each of us found a little goodie on our cot that Nita had shared from one of the few packages she received.

Pfc. Gladys Trask had been a librarian in the public school system of La Grange, Illinois. She was in her mid-thirties, somewhat proper but neither prim nor hypocritical. Gladys had firm, well-reasoned opinions that she usually kept to herself but didn't hesitate to express if the occasion demanded it. She also had the knack of seeing "the forest for the trees," a valuable asset for the work we were doing. She kindly gave me a movie reel of a group of Wacs marching in formation at Fort Des Moines. Gladys, Marge, and Marion formed a usual threesome.

Pvt. Harriott Bell, known as Bell, was the daughter of a Buffalo, New York, judge. She had enlisted upon graduation from Smith College, where she had majored in French. Bell was tall and somewhat stocky and had a pleasing, expressive face and long, dark hair, which she usually wore rolled back from her face because of the dust. Besides her keen intellect—she was a brilliant linguist and extremely well read—I liked her for her tremendous sense of humor, her fun-loving, daring, and adventuresome spirit, and her propensity for attracting incident. In fact, everyone liked Bell.

Pvt. Marion Bowman, who came from Webster, New York, was an ex-librarian. Her personality couldn't be described as exciting or colorful, but she was friendly, loyal, and kindhearted and possessed a logical, sound mind. She could be relied upon in times of adversity.

Pvt. Margery Cady, from Canastota, New York, was an ex-schoolteacher in her early thirties. Gruff, curt, goodhearted, and sensitive, she tended to go along on her own, loyal to the group but rarely socializing with any of us. She had a camera and spent much of her time taking photographs and developing the film. For reasons she never divulged, she destroyed her pictures after the war. Cady was a masterful procurer. She knew where to go—the navy and the Seabees—to acquire pillows, sheets, mattresses, and a variety of food, which she generously gave to friends. She received lots of mail, including packages of goodies, which she also shared readily. Cady's letters provided me with much information regarding dates, places, and material items and were generously given to me along with her complete winter uniform.

Pvt. Maxine "Slapsie Maxie" Clopine, an ex-schoolteacher, was from Red Cloud, Nebraska. When addressing her, we called her Maxine, not because she would have objected to our sobriquet, but because it was simply more convenient. She had dark blonde hair, blue-gray eyes, and a peaches-and-cream complexion (I secretly suspected she didn't take her Atabrine). Only her hooked nose prevented her from being pretty. She was voluptuous and rather sexy. She didn't pal around with anyone in the group.

Pvt. Violet Flower, "Vi" or "Posy," was a graduate of the University of Michigan and had been a biochemist with Dow Chemical when she decided to enlist. Vi was slightly pudgy and had a round face, tiny nose, twinkly blue eyes, and an English accent. She was quiet, didn't party much, and socialized mostly with her tent mates.

Pvt. Beatrice "Bea" Hart, marvelously likeable, was older than the rest of us and barely made it for the fifty-year-old enlistment requirement. She told us she enlisted because she taught school during the daytime and her husband worked nights so they hardly saw enough of each other to get acquainted. She moved slowly, spoke with a drawl, and seemed to perspire perpetually. At Vint Hill I recall her working at advanced cryptanalytic exercises, her face glistening with perspiration. Then the quiet was interrupted by a long sigh and her weary drawl, "Ahve just about reached mah sat-u-ra-tion point." Bea always came up with the appropriate expression.

Pvt. Edith "Mac" McMann was a vivacious, fun-loving, freckle-faced girl of Irish extraction from Arlington, Massachusetts. We loved her accent. She was with us for only about two months in New Guinea when she acquired "jungle rot," lost her eyesight, and had to be sent home.

Pvt. Marjorie Wilhelm left the University of Wisconsin to enlist. At twenty-one, she was the youngest of the group, but she was mature and well informed, especially in history, politics, and literature. Marge was also intelligent, logical, and pragmatic. She could argue heatedly, but she never forced her opinions on others. She was enthusiastic and fun-loving in a refined way, and all of us liked and respected her.